# Ketogen.

# +

# Intermittent Fasting

## 2 books in 1

The complete diet to lose weight fast
and lose weight without hunger.
Food plan and recipes included.

### Claudia Rodriguez

# Summary

# Ketogenic Diet

## The essential guide to burning fat, learning to eat healthy and improving your health

CLAUDIA RODRIGUEZ

# Introduction: Change your life now!

Whenever I wanted to start something new, something different, I would stop. There was almost a force inside me that was blocking me, something I couldn't understand and especially couldn't handle.

I could not understand how I could not achieve the goals I set for myself in life. When I had a goal I was convinced that it was within reach but I could never achieve it. I felt incomplete, unable to do what I really wanted.

For a long period of my life I experienced this situation, when I talked about it with others I would hear the reply, "it's normal, it happens to everyone" ... I didn't know what to think, was it really normal to keep feeling dissatisfied with something that you don't even know what it is? It probably wasn't normal at all, and to realize that, I had to hit my head about it many times. I was dissatisfied with my physique, it certainly wasn't as unwatchable as I told myself, yet the mirror had become my worst enemy. I thought it was really unbelievable, I was almost 30 years old and I was afraid to look at myself in front of a mirror. I remembered when I was little, I loved looking in the mirror, what had happened now to my life? What was keeping me from behaving the way I did in my teenage years? Where had my carefreeness gone?

I was pointing these faults at others, I thought it was never my responsibility, I believed that others were constantly at fault, I did not understand why everyone treated me badly, why no one supported me in my choices. In reality, it was not like that at all, I was the one who was always taking the negative side of others, I could not take responsibility, I was still not aware that all the issues stemmed solely and exclusively from my own choices.

I realized after a while that I was actually not alone, most of the people around me were thinking in exactly the same way without realizing it.

I began to pay more attention to my habits; I absolutely had to figure out what was holding me back, what was really affecting my life. After a week of continuous monitoring and analysis of my activities, I realized something that left me bitterly surprised.

Every day I behaved the same way, nothing really changed, my usual routine was destroying me. Those very same routines had created a comfort zone in which I was moving. I could not get out of it, every time I had the thought of doing something different the fear of getting out of my comfort zone would stop me and I would go back to acting the same way again and again.

I was afraid to change, I was always thinking about the negative side, telling myself that if I did something different I would surely face negative consequences. In reality, these thoughts were only and simply detrimental to me. How could I regain my fitness if I kept eating junk food?

I would not even start new diets because I was convinced from the start that I would give up as always, I was already starting out defeated. In reality I was not lacking anything, it was just my way of thinking that was holding me back drastically.

I had convinced myself that I couldn't do anything different than what I usually did, I didn't think I deserved anything better. Until I hit rock bottom, for the umpteenth morning I once again didn't have the courage to look at myself in the mirror fearing that what I saw I might not like ... I felt like crying, I was tired of this situation, really too tired.

The risk was to fall into a major depressive crisis, on the other hand as the only alternative I had the opportunity to engage and really change.

Remember, too, that without change things will always remain the same and indeed will eventually get worse and die. If you don't decide to change continuously you only risk slumbering in your situation with no way out.

The reality is that most people are afraid to change, unconsciously not wanting to get out of their comfort zone. It can be uncomfortable to change one's eating habits, especially if they are very ingrained. It takes energy and strength to resist change rather than accept it. I assure you that it is much easier to decide to change than to continue being the way you are. It really depends on your choices, though. How do you think many people have managed to lose weight, to lose even more than 20 kilograms, they simply worked hard, they were consistent, they really believed in what they were doing.

Deciding not to change means not experiencing new adventures, new excitement, and sometimes even new love, do you really want to preclude yourself from this? If your physical situation embarrasses you, do you really want to spend your whole life not having the courage to look at yourself in the mirror, put on a bikini to go to the beach, or wear a tight T-shirt? Do you really think you don't deserve to live like everyone else? The truth is that you not only deserve this but you deserve so much more.

Your limits depend only on your thoughts. These are defined by many scholars as mental paradigms, that is, limits that our mind unconsciously sets for itself. Many times we believe that we are unable to do something, in reality maybe we have never tried to do better or we have not really committed ourselves to that area. Fortunately, it is possible to change your paradigms, you have to be aware of these limitations of yours, only then will you be able to overcome them. The time has come to embrace change, you do not have to avoid it, change does not mean getting worse but entering a new mental and physical state that will allow you to live life differently. You will finally be able to experience new emotions, if you do not take risks however, your life will continue to be flat, without stimulation. What is the point of living a life without any stimulation, without appreciating yourself? Remember that your body is the only thing that will be with you forever, throughout your life until you die. Why do you want to keep mistreating it?

Imagine buying a luxurious, unique, priceless car and then soiling the seats with food, breaking the upholstery or destroying the body. That would be something crazy wouldn't it? I bet you think so, now though, explain to me why you act this way with your body. It doesn't make any sense. I was also in this situation, and if I was able to take my life into my own hands, so can you. Really, no one has special powers, there is no magic formula to change, everything depends solely and exclusively on you. Are you willing to change or not? You must answer this question before proceeding with the reading.

I would like this to be more than just a book for you, I would like it to be your traveling companion, the manual that accompanies you in the dark moments, in the difficult moments, when it seems that no one understands what you are feeling. I can assure you that in this book you will always find solutions to your problems, I would like this to inspire you, to change your point of view, to push you forward at the moment when you are about to give up everything and fall back into old habits.

I wish you the best of luck in your future and wish you a good          reading          of          this          lib

# What is the Ketogenic Diet?

One of the most famous and popular diets around the world, especially in recent years, is definitely the Ketogenic diet also known simply as the Keto Diet. According to Google's annual search report, this is among the top ten most searched diets on the web. Why is this diet so sought after? Why are more and more people wanting to follow this diet regimen?

Surely the main reason is that this diet allows people to achieve great results without a major expenditure of energy and especially without mental effort. There are many diets that allow people to lose weight, but they go to a great deal of stress on the psychological side; in fact, they are studded with continuous deprivation of so many types of foods. A diet that stresses the mental side will surely have negative repercussions on the physical side in the long run as well. This is especially the case with all those diets that allow you to lose many kilograms in a very short time with very stringent dietary restrictions, but which lead you after a few weeks to regain it with interest.

Dieto Cheto can be tested by everyone, whether athletes or those who have never played sports in their lives and lead sedentary lives. This is precisely why I decided to tell you about it in this book. In whatever condition you are in fact you can test the benefits derived from this diet.

It has to be said that not everyone likes the Ketogenic diet and perhaps prefers other diets, it is absolutely normal. Each person should adopt the diet regimen that is closest to their lifestyle and way of eating.

The Ketogenic Diet is an eating program that consists of minimizing carbohydrates and increasing fats that will be the source of energy for our body. This diet has also been followed by many physicians such as Scott Keatley of Keatley Medical Nutrition Therapuy.

Obviously each person has different nutritional needs resulting from weight, height, gender but also age. However, in most cases each person applying this diet should introduce into his or her body:

60-75% of calories from consumption of high-fat foods;

15-30% calories from protein;

5-10% calories from carbohydrates.

So as you can see, carbohydrates represent a very low percentage in this diet. When we talk about carbohydrates we refer, for example, to pasta, which is so beloved by us Italians, but also to bread and many other foods.

Generally in this diet you should not eat more than 50 grams each day of carbohydrates, of course there can be small variations, but in most cases this is the rule you should try to follow. During this diet you enter a state of ketosis, and ketones are activated, we will see later what they are. Ketones together with a substance called Beta Hydroxybutyrate help reduce seizures according to much medical research. You should know that initially the Ketogenic diet was intended to help people who had seizure disorders, so its purpose was certainly not to make people lose weight.

However as more and more people tried this diet they realized that you could lose even many kilograms in a healthy and balanced way. This happens because when you eat carbohydrates, reactions develop in your body that cause it to retain fluids that will be used to store carbohydrates that will be used to produce energy. When you don't ingest a lot of carbohydrates, your body retains less fluid, for these very reasons you will lose weight much more easily.

Very often, however, we eat a lot of carbohydrates, almost without realizing it, which is precisely why we cannot control our weight and gain weight. If, however, there are foods in the diet that are rich in fats, these can help curb the cravings that lead us to assimilate large amounts of these foods. In fact, fatty foods provide satisfaction and prevent the creation of that feeling of "lack," of emptiness in the person.

# Ketosis

The moment you follow this diet after about seven days a natural process called ketosis will be activated. This process is initiated by the body because it helps it survive when food intake is low. Don't worry with this I am not telling you that this is a dangerous diet, far from it, however I am explaining how it acts on our body. We do not manage these processes but they are activated automatically. During the state of Ketosis, so-called Ketones are produced through the breakdown of fats in the liver.

When your body is in this metabolic state, it starts burning fat, this allows you to lose weight fast. You have to know that our body adapts to the food we eat, when it is overloaded with fat and no more carbohydrates are introduced, it starts to burn ketones as its primary energy source. When this happens there are very important benefits both for weight loss but also for health itself and for physical and mental performance.

In fact, it is no secret that a great many sportsmen and women follow this diet to enable their bodies to do better and better and improve their performance.

## How to enter a state of ketosis?

Surely now you are wondering how to enter a state of ketosis, that is, that body condition that allows you to lose a lot of weight in a very short time. The first thing you will have to do is definitely to limit carbohydrates, as mentioned earlier, this is a really crucial aspect. You should ingest a maximum of 50gr a day, but if you want even faster results this quota could go down to 35gr a day. Obviously these are just recommendations based on my readings and experience, in all cases it would be preferable to consult a doctor before implementing too drastic choices. When I give these examples I am referring to a person in perfect health and of average body weight, if you are in a particular physical condition you should still consult an expert.

Another very important aspect is definitely limiting protein intake. In fact, it is no secret that a lot of protein can lead to lower levels of ketosis. You should eat on average 0.6 to 0.8 grams of protein for every kilogram of your body and then divide the result by two. In all cases you can easily find gram calculators on the Internet in relation to your weight and height for the Keto diet.

Don't worry about fat. Remember that this is the main source of energy. Make sure you get enough nutrition; you don't have to go hungry on the Ketogenic diet. As in any diet regimen, don't forget to drink enough water. A liter of water a day can really make a difference. So make sure you hydrate yourself and stay consistent with the amount of water you drink. Water allows you to regulate many vital functions of your body, but it also has another very interesting function, namely, it allows you to better control your toxin elimination levels resulting in better cellular renewal by your body.

One of the biggest problems, however, that concerned me and I realized that it is also proper to a lot of other people was definitely snacking. In fact, I kept eating food even when it was actually not necessary. For example, out of boredom I would eat a brioche or chips or tarallini or even toast with Nutella. These snacks that were not absolutely necessary made my weight rise and made me lose control of my life. Without realizing it, I was constantly putting a strain on my body, which needed the right amounts of healthy foods throughout the day. Weight loss in fact improves when you have few insulin spikes during the day. Every time you eat food there are insulin spikes, and if these are not needed, this could turn into a problem.

So I learned to avoid these misplaced snacks and rather than eating I devoted myself to taking care of my body by starting to do physical exercises. Exercise, not me but numerous experts say, is definitely healthy for your body. Even 20 to 30 minutes of exercise every day can bring some really amazing results. I am not talking about particularly stressing your physique, especially if you have never done sports, but you could start taking brisk walks or jogs whenever you have free time. This activity allows you to regulate your weight loss and especially your blood sugar levels.

# Benefits of the Ketogenic Diet

There are obvious benefits that people who follow a Ketogenic Diet can enjoy. Obviously, the first benefit that can be recognized is that related to weight loss either through increased metabolism or through reduced appetite sensation.

The foods that are eaten on the ketogenic diet, which I will tell you about later both through recipes and the eating plan, are very satiating and many times reduce the hormones that stimulate hunger. Following such a diet allows you to reduce your appetite and consequently allows you to lose extra pounds. I can tell you for sure, many times I too could not control my hunger feelings and would ingest everything without realizing it. Later I would try to eat healthy and light at lunch and dinner, but those small snacks that I thought were insignificant actually betrayed me. Moreover, sometimes I would be invited to parties where I would continue to eat without following any dietary regimen anymore and I would find myself back to square one.

I was really tired of this situation precisely because of this I decided to try the Ketogenic Diet, for the first time I was not only able to lose weight but also experienced very obvious health benefits that I never expected.

Ketogenic diets in most cases succeed in making the person lose more pounds over time than diets that are very low in fat. Yes, I know this might seem like something that goes against logic, but it absolutely does not.

This greater loss of kg is measured not only in the long run but also after only 6 months. You will lose weight right away, but after a few months you will have lost more kg than any other person on other diets.

The Ketogenic diet also has a high positive impact on acne. In fact, links have been found between the presence of blood sugar and acne. When you have a diet rich in carbohydrates and many of them are also processed and refined, this can alter the balance of bacteria in the gut. This alteration leads to an increase or decrease in blood sugar. These changes in the glycemic index can very negatively affect skin health.

In 2012 a study was done that showed that lower carbohydrate intake could reduce all acne-related symptoms. This is obviously not a magic recipe however it is a dietary regimen that over time can give great results.

What if I told you that a good diet can also positively affect your heart health? When a person follows such a diet, in fact, he or she begins to eat foods that are healthy, that is, that have beneficial effects on the body. Eating fats therefore does not mean eating food that does us harm but far from it, there are fats that are healthy such as those that come from the avocado, which are completely different from those you might eat by ingesting red meat or pork. It seems that people who eat healthy can in fact enjoy a very significant drop in blood cholesterol.

When there are very high levels of cholesterol in the blood, you are at risk of going into cardiovascular disease. You should avoid being in such a situation because you may be headed for some not-so-pleasant complications. Heart health depends on the quality of your diet, this is an opinion shared by a great many experts. Eating healthy, balanced foods will only preserve your health.

The heart is not the only organ in your body that feels the benefits from a healthy diet; in fact, the ketones that are generated during the diet provide benefits to brain function as well. In fact, they can protect the brain and especially nerve cells. These types of diets are also recommended for people who would like to prevent or otherwise manage forms of Alzheimer's disease.

As mentioned in earlier chapters, this diet was also very much adopted initially by all people suffering from seizures. During this dietary regimen we said that you enter a state of ketosis, this can allow people suffering from epilepsy to reduce seizures.

## What should you pay attention to?

As we have seen the Ketogenic diet has very positive effects on human health however there are some things you should watch out for especially if you decide to follow this diet regime in the long run. There could be a risk of an increase in some health problems such as kidney stones, an excess of protein in the blood or even a buildup of fat in the liver.

These are conditions that appear rarely and only if you follow this diet for several years without taking healthy fatty foods and preferring animal foods in any case. Other minor adverse effects could be the following: fatigue, low blood sugar, constipation, headache, nausea. It might happen that some of these symptoms occur only at the beginning of the diet, this happens because the body is not used to this new diet and its energy sources.

There are some people for whom it is not advisable to follow this style of eating, they are those who already have previous issues, such as people with diabetes, those who have eating disorders, who have kidney disease or pancreatitis, and it is also not recommended for pregnant women. If you are not in any of these situations this may be the diet for you.

In all cases, it is best to discuss this dietary regimen with a physician, specifically a dietitian or nutritionist, especially for people who are managing an illness.

# Hormones and the Ketogenic Diet

One of the topics for which there has been much discussion over time concerns the effects of the ketogenic diet on the hormones of us women but also men. Some say that this diet has positive effects regarding hormone regulation while others think that it is not very suitable for this purpose.

Hormones have a very important function in our bodies because they are like chemical messengers that carry information from the endocrine glands that are crucial in regulating all the various processes. Our bodies are really complex machines and every process that occurs is not random but is regulated by a number of factors. Sometimes, however, we can go into a hormonal imbalance that is absolutely not good for our bodies and in fact generates different health problems. Some people think that such a diet can cause these imbalances. In reality, this is not really the case.

Many of people's health problems are related to the insulin hormone. When we consume a lot of carbohydrates more insulin is produced by our body than it should. Of course, this also happens when we ingest a lot of sugar; in fact, glucose sends signals to the body to release insulin. This becomes a problem if insulin is in excess.

For people who frequently eat junk food it happens very frequently that their blood sugar levels are higher than they should be. Many people then contract serious chronic health problems such as type 2 diabetes. To avoid being in this situation one should certainly constantly monitor blood sugar levels or adopt a type of diet that allows the introduction of few sugar- or carbohydrate-rich foods. There is, however, good news for all this, the ketogenic diet is really outstanding for regulating insulin.

Do you know why this happens? Because very few carbohydrates and sugars are introduced on the ketogenic diet. Cortisol is also stimulated when carbohydrates and sugars are eaten. This is released by the kidney glands at the time when our body is under stress. When there is a sudden change in blood sugar level, our body releases cortisol which generates the feelings of stress. With the ketogenic diet, these hormonal surges are not there because we consistently eat food low in carbohydrates and sugar.

The ketogenic diet therefore gives a good response to blood sugar spikes and allows you to reduce that nagging feeling of stress that can suck up a lot of energy. Much less cortisol is released when you follow this diet than when you have an unhealthy diet, this also allows the adrenal glands to relieve stress and return to proper function.

So all the foods that you will read about in the next chapters are much less taxing on your body and definitely improve your metabolism.

When the hormones are out of balance in us women, we might develop a syndrome called PCOS, which is polycystic ovary syndrome. In this case there is an imbalance of reproductive hormones that causes infertility in us women.

Most women who have this syndrome are overweight or obese, and have symptoms related to abnormal insulin values, high blood sugar, or metabolic syndrome.

There is no cure to PCOS, however, many times it is advisable for people suffering from this syndrome to apply a ketogenic diet. This is becoming a very popular and recommended treatment. According to research, women who are in this condition and have followed the ketogenic diet have had very important improvements especially in blood insulin levels.

Finally according to many researches the ketogenic diet has high potential for these women, it can in fact contribute positively to pregnancy outcomes, this diet in fact helps to alleviate all symptoms related to PCOS and improves women's quality of life.

Another very important aspect that is related to hormones is definitely that related to the thyroid gland. When the thyroid gland is out of control it brings a number of problems such as hypothyroidism and very serious autoimmune diseases. Some people who are against this diet think that it can negatively affect the functions of the thyroid gland when in reality we can say that it is absolutely the opposite.

When a person has thyroid problems they should try to act on their immune system. You should know that ketones have very good regulatory functions and many times they help your body to heal the immune system, this sometimes leads to a better hormonal balance, with all the consequences.

Finally, we absolutely must talk about premenstrual syndrome. This is a condition that affects all women on the planet but also indirectly affects men who have to deal with us women. This is the reality. With PMS there are a lot of mood swings, we go from depressive phases to headaches, fatigue, irritability but also food cravings and acne. This list could go on and on. Every woman experiences many different symptoms. I have simply listed the most common ones.

Brace yourself, you should know that the ketogenic diet is an eating regimen that allows you to mitigate these symptoms, and I myself have experienced the benefits on my own skin. In fact, it has a positive effect on many of the symptoms I mentioned                                         earlier.

# Ketogenic Diet and Low Carb Diet

The Ketogenic Diet and the Low Carb Diet, about which I wrote a book that I recommend you read, are very similar to each other but each has different benefits. Choosing one over the other depends mainly on what your goals, lifestyle and preferences are. These diets have some commonalities, in fact for both of them healthy fats, vegetables such as avocados are very important and carbohydrates are kept relatively low.

The ketogenic diet allows you to burn body fat. You will first burn what you eat and then what you have stored. Unlike other diets during the ketosis process you will not be able to eat a lot and you will not be very hungry, because during this phase your hunger is suppressed by the movement of your cells. You may feel full even after eating little, which means you will be able to burn body fat without being hungry all the time.

As I have already explained to you doing a diet that does not heavily affect your psychological side is crucial so that you can avoid unpleasant relapses that will cause you to regain the weight you lost with interest. The other very important benefit is that this diet through the process of ketosis accelerates your metabolism so this allows you to burn more than 300 calories every day.

In summary, you will have the opportunity to burn a lot of calories without going hungry because you will already feel full. This will allow you to lose weight steadily. If you want to reach your goals quickly this may be the diet for you.

In addition, the Ketogenic diet will allow you to have more energy. In fact, your blood sugar concentration can make you feel exhausted or energized. When you consume carbohydrates these affect your blood sugar level. Reducing carbohydrates can help you keep your blood sugar level balanced, giving stability to your energy levels throughout the day.

The ketogenic diet also reduces inflammation, perhaps due to a ketone metabolite called beta-hydroxybutyrate, which has positive effects especially in the case of liver inflammation.

The low-carb diet, on the other hand, is great not only for people who expend a lot of energy and those who want to lose weight but also for people who want to put on muscle mass and do anaerobic activities such as weightlifting or other intense workouts.

Just as in the Ketogenic diet, the low percentage of carbohydrates in the diet will also allow for the balancing of blood glucose especially in case you decide to eat complex carbohydrates rather than simple ones.

Finally, this diet allows you to lose weight but be relaxed at the same time. The Ketogenic diet is stricter because you should never go out of the state of ketosis to lose weight quickly but it allows you to achieve amazing results that are unattainable with other diets. Low carb, on the other hand, allows you to eat your favorite carbohydrates now and then, such as potatoes. In the long run maybe this one would fit best.

As you can see these are two very similar diets, each has its advantages but now it's up to you to decide which one to follow based on your lifestyle as well.

# Shopping list: what to buy at the supermarket

Now that we have seen what the ketogenic diet is, what its benefits are, and why you should do it, let's go over what foods you should buy that are suitable for this type of diet regimen.

These are just suggestions, of course you are free to decide whether to follow them or not. I am not going to tell you about any particular supermarket, but rather they will be foods that you can really find everywhere. This also makes this diet easier to follow.

Let's see together what they are.

## Seafood

There are certain types of fish such as salmon that are perfect for this type of diet. In fact, salmon is rich in certain vitamins such as B vitamins, potassium and selenium and is literally carbohydrate-free, which makes it perfect for this type of diet.

Not all shellfish however are carbohydrate-free, in fact these vary from time to time. Shrimps and crabs generally lack carbohydrates however there are others that do have them, albeit in small amounts. My advice is to evaluate in each case how many carbohydrates you are going to ingest. That way you will have the whole situation under control.

Let me give you an example of the carbohydrate content per

100 grams for some types of shellfish that you can easily find at the fish market or supermarket. Both clams and mussels and octopus per 100 grams contain 4 grams of carbohydrates, oysters and squid on the other hand only 3. So if you have to consume 40 grams of carbohydrates during the day, every little bit can be really important.

With some types of fatty fish such as sardines and mackerel you can get omega-3, which is a key fat for our bodies because it allows us to lower insulin levels. Supplements of omega-3 are also sold, however you can safely find it in the food you eat. Also according to some studies, it would seem that everyone who takes omega-3 has improved cognitive health and is also able to be more focused.

If you could eat at least 3 meals a week of fish, you could get good results. Of course, I know that fish comes at a cost, sometimes a significant cost, and it is for these very reasons that I will talk to you about other foods as well.

## Low-carb vegetables

When we talk about low-carb vegetables, we are referring to non-starchy vegetables that are rich in nutrients as well as vitamin C and other minerals. As you probably know vegetables contain a lot of fiber, your body does not absorb it in the same way as carbohydrates. Therefore to monitor the calculation of carbohydrates to these must be subtracted the fiber introduced into our body, only in this way can you understand the "net" carbohydrates that have been absorbed by your body.

You must be careful, however, not to consume large portions of starchy vegetables such as potatoes, sweet potatoes or beets because you may exceed your (very low) carbohydrate limit for your day. So don't think that because they are vegetables you can eat them in industrial quantities; you should always consider the carbohydrates your body absorbs.

Some recommended non-starchy vegetables are, for example, Brussels sprouts or spinach. In addition, these contain antioxidants to help protect cells and prevent them from being damaged.

Another vegetable you could definitely buy is cauliflower, which can often also be used as a substitute for rice or mashed potatoes. In the October/November period, pumpkin can also be your good ally. You can prepare numerous dishes with it and it contains very few carbohydrates, so eating healthy certainly does not mean sacrificing taste.

You just need to change your outlook and figure out what healthy foods you should be eating.

This is precisely why I recommend other vegetables that you could include in your eating plan that are very low in carbohydrates: cucumbers, cabbage, asparagus, green beans, eggplant, lettuce, olives, peppers, tomatoes, zucchini.

## Avocado

Regarding this vegetable it is definitely necessary to talk about it in a separate paragraph. Avocados in fact have extremely positive effects on your body even though they contain carbohydrates, so you should not eat more than you should. On average, one avocado per 100 grams contains 9 grams of carbohydrates. You should know that 7 of these 9 grams of carbohydrates are fiber, so the amount of net carbohydrates, influencing your diet, is 2 per 100 grams.

This food is rich in vitamins like all other vegetables but also in a very important mineral for the human body such as potassium. The higher amount of potassium in our body allows us to enter the ketosis phase faster and thus to lose weight. It is also very important in bringing cholesterol and triglycerides in our body into balance.

Some people strongly believe that there are long-term benefits to eating one avocado a day. Avocados, if you've never had them, have a very distinctive taste that goes well with both fruit but also with salmon or eggs.

The cost of avocados compared to other fruits or vegetables is slightly higher in Italian supermarkets, however, you should not buy them in large quantities, even a little a day can be good for your body.

## Meat

If you are not a vegan or vegetarian, you should never go without the energy intake from eating meat. Meat, especially chicken meat, contains no carbohydrates and is as rich in vitamins as the other foods I have told you about in this chapter.

Obviously meat is an excellent source of protein that also helps to improve your muscle mass while consuming a very low carbohydrate content. It cannot be compared to fish however, again its effects are very positive.

In all cases it is preferable to eat meat that does not come from intensive farming, because animals that simply eat grass and are left to graze certainly produce more omega-3s than others and also more antioxidants. Many times this kind of meat is sold at a slightly higher price than average, however in health terms it is worth spending a little more.

## Cheeses

In many diets, actually in most, the consumption of cheeses is strictly forbidden because they are high-fat foods. In the ketogenic diet, however, these can be eaten because the foods to be avoided are those that are high in carbohydrates. Therefore, cheeses shape up as an ideal food for the ketogenic diet.

Typically for every 30 grams of cheese (a general average) there are 1 gram of carbohydrates and 6.5 grams of protein.

Cheese contains conjugated linoleic acid, which is nothing but a fat that helps improve body composition. In addition, according to some studies, cheese is a food that helps reduce cell aging and maintain muscle mass.

So let's take a look at the cheeses you could use in your ketogenic diet: Brie, Cheddar (the American one), Camembert, cottage cheese, goat cheese, feta, mascarpone, mozzarella, parmesan, provolone, romano, string cheese, Swiss, halloumi.

## Olive oil

In our Italian food culture, Olive Oil certainly cannot be missing. Every day it is used in many meals. Olive oil that is produced in Italy is rich in oleic acid, this is a fat that has been shown in several studies to reduce the possibility of heart disease.

This is not the end of the story, because in extra virgin olive oil there are many antioxidants such as phenols that protect heart health by decreasing various inflammations. This oil contains no carbohydrates but is rich in pure fats. You can use it for salad dressings, or even when you eat fish or you can put a drizzle of olive oil on meat or with vegetables. It goes well with any kind of food, it really is a must-have food in your diet.

The only advice I can give you is to use it mainly in low-temperature cooking, because some of its properties may be lost with high temperatures.

## Coconut oil

After talking about olive oil, we surely cannot fail to refer to coconut oil as well. It is certainly much less used in our dietary regime than olive oil, however the benefits that this oil brings to our body are also very important. It has a different taste than olive oil and does not go well with all foods, however with this you can create very tasty dishes.

As mentioned, it has very important properties that make it unique especially in such a diet. This oil contains medium-chain fats that are absorbed by the liver and converted into ketones.

In fact, this oil is used to increase the level of ketones in the body and thus accelerate the process of ketosis.

# Nuts and seeds

These are also healthy foods and especially rich in fat. Consistently consuming nuts can reduce the risk of heart disease, and also reduce the risk of being a victim of some types of cancer. I want to make it clear that these foods are not cures for these diseases but can only help prevent them.

These foods are rich in fiber, which can help improve satiety. They are generally low in net carbohydrates and taste great, which is precisely why they are so popular.

Let's see what nuts and seeds you could buy: cashews, almonds, macadamia nuts, Brazil nuts, pistachios, pecans, walnuts, chia seeds, pumpkin seeds, flax seeds, sesame seeds.

These foods also may allow a slowing of aging.

# Eggs

Eggs are a very healthy food and also very versatile because they are present in so many diets and pair well with so many foods. For this reason they should never be missing from your Ketogenic diet, unless you are a vegan. In the latter case we will look at some good alternatives.

One large egg contains less than 1 gram of carbohydrates and 6 grams of protein, so very important nutritional values especially for those leading a ketogenic diet.

Eggs also give a feeling of fullness and satiety. However, it is advisable to eat the whole egg rather than the scrambled egg because most of its nutritious properties are found in the yolk.

# Coffee and tea without sugar

Yes, in this diet you can drink coffee and tea without any problem. These are drinks that are carbohydrate-free. Many Italians and even I could not do without my coffee every morning, which allowed me to wake up faster. Fortunately on the ketogenic diet it is possible to drink it. Coffee is rich in caffeine, a substance that increases metabolism and can also improve physical performance but also mood. In fact, there are even supplements that contain caffeine. Caffeine is also present in some drinks such as RedBull, however these are high in sugar so they are absolutely not recommended, as are other sugar-rich carbonated drinks and you should avoid drinking them when following this diet.

Those who consistently drink coffee and tea, without sugar, also seem much more unlikely to fall victim to diabetes. Try to avoid drinks that are called "zero fat" because in most cases they contain substances and flavorings that are rich in carbohydrates and therefore have nothing to do with this diet.

So if you have always been drinking sugary drinks, I suggest you give up this bad habit because it does not benefit either your weight or your health.

# Dark chocolate and cocoa powder

Many people do not know that dark chocolate and cocoa powder are foods that are present in many athletes' diets. These two foods are excellent antioxidants also have a low carbohydrate content. Its antioxidant properties can be compared to those of any fruit, such as blueberries and acai berries.

Dark chocolate therefore can be an integral part of the Ketogenic diet, however it is very important that this contains at least 70% solid cocoa, and also it is definitely advisable to eat it in moderation without overdoing it. In 30 grams of sugar-free chocolate there are 3 grams of net carbohydrates, so 10 percent.

## Olives

If you are looking for a food that gives you the same benefits that you can find in olive oil, olives are the one for you. Olives contain oleuropein, which is an antioxidant that has anti-inflammatory properties and functions to protect against cell damage.

According to some studies also, olives may be good for bones and blood pressure. Obviously the carbohydrate content changes depending on the size of the olive, however, one must consider that half of their carbohydrates are nothing but fiber, so the net carbohydrates are very low. Just think that about 10 olives contain about 2 grams of carbohydrates, of which 1 gram is fiber.

## Greek yogurt and cottage cheese

Greek yogurt but also cottage cheese are healthy foods that are present in many diets including the Ketogenic diet and are definitely rich in protein. They contain some carbohydrates however they can be included in this dietary regimen. Certainly, however, one should not go overboard in consuming these foods. One must always act in moderation.

About 100 grams of natural Greek yogurt provides 4 grams of carbohydrates and 9 grams of protein. While for 100 grams of cottage cheese there are 5 grams of carbohydrates and 11 of protein. Greek yogurt is therefore slightly lighter than cottage cheese.

These foods fit well into diets because they allow you to reduce the feeling of appetite and most importantly make you feel full. They are also very tasty, especially cottage cheese. Finally, they also combine very well with nuts, cashews, cinnamon and other spices.

## Butter and cream

Many people wonder whether butter and cream can fit into a ketogenic diet. The common thought might be that they have nothing to do with a healthy eating plan these foods. They are actually rich in good fats that can be included in a Keto diet. These are almost carbohydrate-free but have a lot of fats precisely why it is important that you calibrate their daily consumption well.

For a long time these foods were considered to be the cause of the onset of some heart diseases. In fact, numerous studies have shown that moderate consumption of these has nothing to do with such diseases.

These are dairy products that are rich in conjugated linoleic acid, which is nothing but a fatty acid that can promote fat loss.

## Berries

Among the foods to be mentioned are definitely berries. Berries unlike other fruits, which are high in carbohydrates and therefore cannot be included in the ketogenic diet, are an exception. In fact, berries are low in carbohydrates and high in fiber. This makes them perfect for the ketogenic diet. The fiber also allows this food to be highly digestible.

They are all fruits that are very rich in antioxidants that can be very helpful in reducing inflammation and protecting against certain diseases. On average, for every 100 grams of berries there are 7 to 10 grams of carbohydrates. Berries you could buy at any supermarket that would go well with this diet are: blackberries, blueberries, raspberries, and strawberries.

# 21-day food plan

In this chapter I have tried to gather all the information I have to create a 21-day eating plan that you can easily follow. Each day is divided into breakfast, lunch and dinner. If you have a pressing need to snack, I still recommend that you consume in moderate portions one of the foods I mentioned in the previous chapter.

In addition, if you do intense sports activity, I recommend that you take in a slightly higher percentage of carbohydrates than your daily limit, especially before your workout, so that you can have the energy you need to perform at your best.

I applied this food plan on myself and noticed results immediately. I tried to diversify it day by day so that this cannot be boring. You can make some variations, you can consume one meal on one day rather than another. The important thing is not to consume carbohydrate-rich foods. In the next chapter I will also recommend some very tasty recipes that you can include as you like in this food plan instead of foods you are not crazy about.

This food plan is not for vegans or vegetarians, however as I told you, you can use variations for all those dishes that contain foods you prefer not to eat.

Let us see together then what it is all about.

## Week 1

You could start the week, then Monday, with a nice energy

boost. You could eat scrambled eggs for breakfast, which as we mentioned contain very few net carbohydrates. Later for lunch you could eat a bowl of salad with tomatoes and shredded beef. You could also drizzle a little olive oil over the salad. For dinner, a chicken breast with lemon or with spices that can be very helpful in flavoring it.

On the second day for breakfast you could prepare cheese rolls with some small amounts of spices, and for lunch you could prepare a frittata caprese, that is, an egg omelet with mozzarella cheese, cherry tomatoes and also a drop of extra virgin olive oil. Finally for dinner a crispy Keto schnitzel, that is, a breaded schnitzel with walnuts, parmesan cheese and grana cheese.

For Wednesday you could prepare an omelet with fresh spinach for breakfast to get a boost of energy during the morning. For lunch you could cook a chicken soup while in the evening a baked salmon with asparagus.

On Thursday for breakfast you can make a smoothie of milk (lactose-free) and dark chocolate; you can also add a nut or cocoa granola on top. For lunch a big salad with avocado, bacon, and goat cheese, and in the evening some baked flatbreads (you can see the recipe in the next chapter).

On Friday you can make a mushroom omelet for breakfast. For lunch you can have a nice plate of smoked salmon and finally for dinner pork with salad.

On Saturday you can have mascarpone cream, cocoa and almonds for breakfast. For lunch some zucchini stuffed with meat and finally for dinner a sea bream.

On Sunday you can prepare for a sweet breakfast pancakes with berries and whipped cream. For lunch a typical Italian dish, prosciutto, mozzarella, cherry tomatoes, salad and olive oil. Finally for dinner pork chops with green beans and garlic butter or salted butter.

# Week 2

To start the second week on the right foot, since Monday is considered by many to be the heaviest day, you could prepare something sweet and very tasty such as a Yogurt and Blueberry Mousse (you can find the recipe in the next chapter). For lunch you could have a tuna salad with hard-boiled eggs and cherry tomatoes, and for dinner hamburger patties with tomato sauce.

On the second day you could have coffee for breakfast or a cup of green tea, for lunch a plate of roast beef and cheddar or another type of cheese you prefer. For dinner, on the other hand, you could cook grilled salmon with broccoli and cheese; you could also add a little lemon and a drop of oil for flavor.

On Wednesday you can start your day by making coconut porridge for breakfast, a nice plate of hard-boiled eggs, artichokes, shrimp and salad for lunch, and finally crispy chicken nuggets for dinner.

On Thursdays for breakfast you can make egg muffins, for lunch cauliflower soup with crumbled bacon, and finally for dinner baked keto broccoli filanti (find the recipe in the next chapter).

On Fridays for breakfast you can have hard-boiled eggs, and

if you like you can add mayonnaise as well, although I know it might be a bit heavy in the early morning or you might prefer low-fat ham with sottilette. For lunch you can have a Caesar Salad, which is very popular especially with Americans, and for dinner some baked keto chips (find the recipe in the next chapter).

On Saturday you can have an English breakfast with bacon and eggs, for lunch you can have avocados stuffed with salmon, and finally for dinner a steak with baked vegetables.

Finally on Sunday, the last day of the week, you can have for breakfast an omelet with bacon bits, for lunch asparagus wrapped in ham and goat cheese, and finally for dinner cod accompanied by lemon spinach.

## Week 3

You can start the week by eating a whole natural white Greek yogurt for breakfast. For lunch you can have a salad of octopus and green and black olives, and for dinner a grilled turkey breast accompanied by red radicchio and a drizzle of extra virgin olive oil.

On Tuesdays, on the other hand, you can drink a mug of whole milk accompanied also by some nuts. For lunch some low-fat cottage cheese with green salad and tomatoes. Finally, for dinner hard-boiled eggs, boiled artichokes (even those you find in the frozen food aisle are fine) and a drizzle of extra virgin olive oil.

On Wednesday for breakfast you could make orange juice and also eat sugar-free muesli. Instead, for lunch a steamed cod and steamed zucchini. Finally, for dinner you could eat stewed beans accompanied by fennel with extra virgin olive oil.

On Thursday you can have whole Greek white yogurt for breakfast, marinated anchovies and grilled eggplant for lunch, and finally for dinner a grilled sirloin of veal accompanied by red radicchio and as always extra virgin olive oil.

On Friday for breakfast you could have hard-boiled eggs, for lunch a cauliflower and broccoli salad and finally for dinner horse carpaccio, lettuce and extra virgin olive oil.

On Saturday for breakfast you could make a smoothie of low-fat yogurt and dark chocolate, for lunch some grilled chicken breast with lemon and pepper accompanied by fresh lettuce, and finally in the evening for dinner a sea bream with extra virgin olive oil and boiled spinach.

Finally on Sunday, we arrived at the last day of this diet period. For breakfast you could have a yogurt and blueberry mousse, for lunch baked salmon with crispy vegetables, and finally for dinner bresaola baskets with cream cheese, the recipe for which you will find in the next chapter.

## Snacks

On all these days you could eat snacks such as a piece of grana cheese, bresaola, ham, nuts, peanuts, cashews, dried fruits, almonds, clementines. You decide what to eat during the diet days, the important thing is that you can avoid all excesses.

# Recipes for the Ketogenic Diet

Below I will present some recipes for the ketogenic diet that are very easy to execute, as far as the seasonings to be used I recommend that you always use as salt the Pink Dell'Himalaya salt, my recommendation is in fact to buy this type of salt in both the "fine" and "coarse" versions and substitute it for ordinary table salt.

In fact, Himalayan pink salt is not refined and is never treated with any process where chemicals are used, and it also remains by its nature free of the pollutants that can instead contaminate types of salt that come from seas and oceans.

It also reduces water retention and hypertension because its sodium chloride content is significantly lower than ordinary table salt. So although the cost is a little higher than ordinary salt, it is worth buying.

As for the oil, I recommend that you always use a good evo oil, that is, extra virgin olive oil, and when I use the abbreviation evo oil it will be to indicate precisely extra virgin olive oil.

## Quick breakfast ideas

-50 grams of smoked salmon with Philadelphia-type spreadable cheese inside

-2 omelet eggs with two sottilette pieces inside, or cook the eggs in a nonstick pan and melt two sottilette pieces on top of the eggs

-A glass of whole milk about 200ml and a small slice of whole grain rye bread with bresaola and cream cheese spread

-One whole Greek yogurt + one small slice of whole grain rye bread with ham and pickle

## Quick lunch ideas:

-Egg salad + arugula + avocado + sunflower seeds

-One mozzarella cheese with fresh spinach in a salad with chopped ripe cherry tomatoes and sunflower seeds

-Salad with salad of your choice + chopped green apple +stemmed celery stick + white grapes and chopped walnuts

-Steamed or grilled cod with grilled or pan-fried zucchini + half an apple

Grilled or steamed octopus accompanied by grilled or cooked eggplant in nonstick pan + half a pear

## Quick snack ideas:

-A handful of walnuts or almonds

-1 cube about 30g parmesan or grana padano cheese

-1 hard-boiled egg

- 1 celery rib with 30 g cream cheese spread

## Quick dinner ideas:

-A slice of grilled tuna or salmon with steamed vegetables

-Grilled chicken breast with green salad + half apple or half pear

-Grilled turkey breast with grilled radicchio

# Quick and easy recipes for the Ketogenic diet:

## Stuffed onions

Ingredients:

- 2 large red onions
- 180 g drained tuna in oil
- 2 tablespoons capers
- 2 tablespoons of Gaeta olives
- 1 tablespoon grated pecorino cheese
- parsley
- salt and pepper

Preparation:

Wash the onions and then gently separate the leaves without breaking them. In a bowl mix tuna with pecorino cheese, chopped parsley, chopped olives and capers, salt, pepper. Stuff the onion leaves with the mixture and lay them on a baking sheet lined with baking paper, drizzle with olive oil, bake and cook for 10 min. at 180°. Onions au gratin are a great summer appetizer and are good both hot and cold. If you like you can accompany them with a parsley dip, a walnut dip or a Greek yogurt, herb and garlic dip!

# Cream of cauliflower soup with walnuts olives and bacon

Ingredients:

- ½ head of cauliflower
- 4 walnuts
- 1 tablespoon roasted pine nuts
- 1 clove of garlic
- 2 eggs
- 1 tablespoon taggiasca olives
- 60 g smoked bacon
- pecorino cheese flakes
- chili
- salt and pepper

Preparation:

Wash the cauliflower and divide the florets into smaller pieces then blanch them in salted water flavored with the garlic clove for about 8 min.

Boil the eggs by adding 1 tablespoon vinegar to the water for about 7 min. Meanwhile, cut the bacon into strips and brown it in a pan with chili for a few minutes.

Drain cauliflower and transfer to a blender cup, blend with cooking water adding it according to desired consistency and adjust salt and pepper. Peel the eggs and cut them into wedges then serve the velouté by adding two ladles of velouté to the bottom of the plate, crispy bacon on top, eggs, dried fruit, flaked pecorino cheese, olives, a sprinkle of freshly ground pepper and a drizzle of raw evo oil!

# Keto chicken salad

Ingredients:

- 150 g of grilled chicken
- green salad of your choice
- a stalk of celery
- an onion
- 1 tuft of fresh parsley
- 1 hard-boiled egg
- 2 cloves of minced garlic if liked
- 20 g mayonnaise
- one teaspoon of mustard
- salt and pepper
- one tablespoon of evo oil

Preparation:

chop up the celery stalk the onion and parsley, put everything in a large salad bowl and mix it together with the chopped hard-boiled egg, add the chopped garlic if you like, mayonnaise and mustard and season with the evo oil salt and pepper and add the green salad.

Then add the previously griddled shredded chicken and arrange it in the 'salad bowl with the already prepared dressing and salad and mix it all together.

# Baked salmon with crispy vegetables

Ingredients:

- 2 slices of fresh or frozen salmon
- 2 medium green zucchini
- 1 carrot
- 1/2 onion
- Salt, pepper and olive oil as much as needed

Preparation:

Take a baking sheet and cover it with baking paper and then arrange the salmon fillets on top.

Then wash and chop all the vegetables, zucchini carrots and onion and sauté them in a nonstick pan with a drizzle of oil for about 3 to 4 minutes on high heat, then let cool and add salt and pepper and cover the salmon with the vegetables creating a layer of about 2cm.

Add a drizzle of evo oil on top of the preparation and finally bake for about 20 minutes in an oven already preheated to 180 degrees.

# Crispy chicken keto chunks

Ingredients:

- 2 chicken breasts
- ½ onion
- a tuft of fresh parsley
- fresh or dried rosemary
- 1 whole egg
- almond or walnut flour
- lemon wedges
- salt and pepper to taste

Preparation:

Chop the chicken into bite-sized pieces, then cut the onion into small pieces and add some rosemary and parsley.

Then in a bowl combine the chicken morsels with the onion, rosemary and parsley and season with salt and pepper. Dip the chicken in the previously beaten egg and coat the morsels in almond or walnut flour.

Take a nonstick baking sheet and cover it with baking paper and bake in the previously preheated oven at 180 degrees until golden brown, accompany the morsels garnished with lemon wedges with green salad and tomatoes.

# Keto cauliflower and broccoli salad with smoked bacon

Ingredients:

- 1 broccoli
- 1 cauliflower
- 100 g diced smoked bacon type bacon
- 8 fresh chopped cherry tomatoes
- ½ fresh chopped cucumber
- ½ fresh chopped onion
- 1 teaspoon oregano
- Mayonnaise if you like
- Olive oil, white wine vinegar salt and pepper to taste

Preparation:

Cut the cauliflower and broccoli into small pieces and cook them in boiling water for about 5 minutes.

Meanwhile brown the diced bacon in a pan, let it cool then combine it with the boiled broccoli and cauliflower, add the tomatoes, cucumbers, onion mayonnaise if you like and season with salt, pepper oil and oregano and a drizzle of white wine vinegar.

# Bresaola keto baskets with cream cheese

Ingredients:

- 150 g bresaola
- 100 g cow's ricotta cheese,
- 100 g robiola cheese,
- 1 tablespoon grated Parmesan cheese,
- chopped parsley and basil
- Pitted green olives to taste.
- a few basil leaves,
- salt and pepper

Preparation:

Drain the ricotta so that the watery part is lost, then in a bowl mix the robiola, ricotta and grated grana cheese. Add the salt and pepper. Now add the chopped herbs to the mixture and mix well, then take the bresaola slices and fill each slice with a little of the cheese mousse.

Stick the slice on one side with a toothpick then add the olive and close the basket by sticking the other side of the bresaola slice.

Continue until you run out of ingredients, you can accompany the dish with mixed salad.

# Keto chicken chunks with feta and zucchini

Ingredients:

- 150 gr chicken
- 60 gr diced feta cheese
- 1 zucchini
- 4 basil leaves
- oil, salt and pepper

Preparation:

Cut the chicken into cubes about 1/2 inch thick and place in a bowl to marinate with a drizzle of oil, a pinch of salt pepper and chopped basil leaves. Let stand for about 10 minutes or so.

Cut the zucchini into rounds that are not too thin and brown it in a pan for 6 to 8 minutes with a drizzle of oil and a pinch of salt.

Cook the chicken by sautéing it in a nonstick skillet until it is lightly browned.

Arrange in a cube dish creating a bed of zucchini then joining the chicken cubes and feta, add a drizzle of raw evo oil to taste.

# Keto zucchini stuffed with meat and cheese

Ingredients for 2 persons:

- 4 Round zucchini (or regular zucchini)
- 200 g of lean mince
- 50 gr of grana padano cheese
- 30 gr of Pecorino Romano cheese
- 30 g breadcrumbs
- 1 bunch of fresh basil
- 1 whole egg
- 1 clove of garlic minced if liked
- 1 pinch of salt

Preparation:

Cut the top cap off the zucchini, empty them of their flesh and set aside.

Blanch the zucchini in salted boiling water for a few minutes, they should be soft but not flaky, then drain and lay them on top of a clean tea towel and let cool. In a bowl combine the whole egg previously beaten with a fork, add salt a drizzle of oil, parmesan and pecorino cheese, breadcrumbs and garlic if you like, also add the shredded zucchini flesh, and chopped basil, with your hands or with a mixer create a thick mixture with which to stuff the zucchini.

Stuff the zucchini and bake at 200 degrees for about 30 minutes. Remove from the oven and let cool a few minutes before serving.

# Parmesan keto pies on tomato sauce

Ingredients for 4 cupcakes:

- 2 eggs
- 100 g grated grana padano or parmesan cheese
- 1 tablespoon of flour about 10 g
- 120 ml of cream
- 50 ml of milk
- salt and pepper to taste
- For the sauce:
- 10 tablespoons of fresh tomato sauce
- 1 level tablespoon of evo oil
- salt and pepper to taste
- half onion
- fresh basil leaves

Preparation:

Put the cream in a nonstick saucepan and dilute it with a tablespoon of water, then add the flour stirring well always in the same direction being careful not to let lumps form, add a pinch of salt and bring to a boil.

Whisk the whole eggs and slowly add the Parmesan cheese, then add the cream previously brought to a boil, to the egg and cheese mixture.

Then fill disposable aluminum ramekins previously greased well, preferably with a little butter or olive oil.

Place the 4 aluminum ramekins in a baking dish previously filled 2/3 full with 'water and bake in a bain-marie oven at 180 degrees for about 25 minutes.

For the sauce lightly wilt the onion in a small nonstick pan with oil and a trickle of water, add the tomato sauce salt and pepper if you like and basil and cook for 10 minutes, diluting with water.

When cooked, arrange a few spoonfuls of sauce on the plates underneath and then invert the cupcakes, being careful not to break them when removing them from the molds, serve them piping hot garnishing with a few leaves of fresh basil to taste.

# Zucchini lasagnetta with prosciutto and provolone cheese

Ingredients:

- 3 zucchini
- 200 g sliced provolone cheese
- 2 ounces of sliced cooked ham
- 2 tablespoons of grated parmesan cheese
- fresh thyme
- 1 yolk
- salt and pepper

Preparation:

Wash the zucchini thoroughly then dry them, cut them lengthwise with a mandoline or by hand with a knife so that they are 4 mm thick.

Take a mold and line it with baking paper then lay a first layer of zucchini slices slightly overlapping each other. Arrange slices of provolone cheese on top and then a layer of ham slices, a sprinkling of Parmesan cheese, salt, pepper and some chopped thyme, continue alternating the ingredients until you finish them.

As the last layer, spread an egg yolk and parmesan cheese, bake at 200° for about 20 min. until golden brown and serve!

For this recipe you can substitute zucchini with slices of grilled eggplant and ham with speck or prosciutto, also provolone cheese can be substituted with smoked scamorza or mozzarella cheese loaf!

# Crispy keto cutlet

Ingredients:

- 1 slice of veal 150 g approx.
- 40 g grated parmesan or grana cheese
- 40 g hazelnuts
- 1 whole egg
- evo oil, salt and pepper

Preparation:

Coarsely chop the hazelnuts and combine them with the grated parmesan or grana cheese.

Put the whole egg in a bowl and beat it with a fork and then dip the meat into it on both sides and then later mash it over the parmesan and hazelnut batter.

Heat a nonstick skillet with plenty of evo oil and cook the meat, turning several times, for about 10 minutes. Dry the cutlet from excess oil with kitchen paper.

Serve hot after salting and accompany with grilled zucchini or eggplant.

# Baked stringy keto broccoli

Ingredients:

- 2 Broccoli
- 30 g of slivered almonds
- 3 tablespoons Olive oil
- Salt and pepper to taste
- 2 shredded subcutlets
- 30 g grated parmesan or grana cheese
- one clove of garlic, minced if liked

Preparation:

Cut the broccoli into florets, then wash them under running water and blanch them for 5 minutes in boiling salted water. Drain and let cool, then grease an ovenproof dish with oil and lay the broccoli seasoned with salt, pepper and a drizzle of olive oil and garlic if you like.

Then sprinkle the surface with grated parmesan or grana cheese and chopped sottilette add almond slivers and bake in a 200°C oven for 20 minutes.

# Baked keto crushes

Ingredients for 6 pieces:

- 220 g mozzarella for pizza
- 60 g Philadelphia
- 40 g green or black sliced olives
- 1 teaspoon baking powder for savory
- 2 whole eggs
- 50 g of slivered almonds

Preparation:

Beat the whole eggs with a fork and add the slivered almonds the olives and the baking powder and mix everything together.

Melt the mozzarella and Philadelphia cheese in the microwave for 2 minutes and add them to the eggs with the olives and almonds and add the baking powder and mix well.

Create 6 crushes with the dough and place them spaced apart on a baking sheet and bake at 200 degrees for about 20 minutes.

# keto cloud sandwich

Ingredients:

- 2 egg whites
- 1 whole egg
- 60 gr of light philadelphia
- 1 pinch of salt
- 3 g of instant yeast

Preparation:

Whisk the egg whites with the baking powder, and in another bowl mix the cheese with the egg.

Gently combine the 2 mixtures together, taking care not to let the egg whites disassemble. Form 5 buns and bake in a ventilated oven at 180°C for about 10 to 15 minutes. Let cool for a few minutes and accompany these delicious nonbread sandwiches being actually carb-free to your keto dishes or stuff them with, for example:

-100 g lean cooked ham

-100 g of grilled chicken breast

-2 slices of low-fat cheese or sottilette

-rucola or spinach or tomato or any of the recommended vegetables you prefer.

# Slices of ham with mushrooms

Ingredients:

- 4 slices of fresh ham
- 8 champignon mushrooms
- 2 nuts of ghee butter
- 1 cup broth
- 1 clove of garlic
- Fresh herbs thyme, rosemary, sage
- ½ cup cooking cream
- 1 tablespoon grated parmesan cheese
- salt and pepper

Preparation:

Clean the mushrooms by removing excess soil with a damp cloth and cutting off the end of the stem then cut them into thin slices of about half an inch.

Melt the butter in a saucepan and brown the garlic, add the mushrooms and let them wilt for a few min. over moderate heat with a lid.

When cooked, remove the mushrooms from the pan and set them aside, in the same pan brown the ham slices on both sides and then add the broth, let the meat cook on a low flame for about 10 min. with a lid.

When the meat is cooked, add the mushrooms and cream and turn up the heat for 1-2 min. so that the cream thickens.

Add the Parmesan cheese and chopped herbs, season with salt and pepper and stir to season then serve the dish hot!

You can use chicken breast, turkey breast, drumsticks or slices of beef in place of ham for this recipe. Also try it with rabbit meat, it is delicious!

# Catalan cream keto

Ingredients:

- 250 ml whipping cream
- 250 gr mascarpone
- 4 egg yolks
- 1 vanilla pod or vanilla powder
- 50 gr erythritol for sweetening

Preparation:

Dip the vanilla pod or vanilla powder into the liquid cream and boil.

Beat the egg yolks with electric whips and add the erythritol and mascarpone while continuing to mix.

Add the cream to the mixture after letting it cool a little and removing the vanilla pod if you preferred it to vanilla powder.

Put the created mixture into six souffle molds and place them in a baking dish filled with water to cover 1/3 of the molds.

Bake at 180 degrees for 50 minutes. Remove from oven and let cool and store in refrigerator, before serving sprinkle with a teaspoon of erythritol and burn with a burner to create a golden crust.

# Avocado celery and mint smoothie

Ingredients:

- 1 avocado
- 2 ribs of celery
- 1 lime
- 2 cm ginger root
- 1 tablespoon chia seeds
- 300 milliliters of coconut milk
- fresh mint leaves

Preparation:

Peel the avocado, remove the inner pit and cut it into pieces.

Wash the celery ribs and remove the hard filaments by pulling them away with a knife.

Peel the lime and remove the skin from the ginger then put all the ingredients in a blender and operate until smooth.

If you prefer a smoother consistency, add water.

If you like, you can replace the celery with another vegetable and the spearmint with any aromatic herb!

# Frequently asked questions about the Ketogenic Diet

In this chapter I have collected all the most frequently asked questions concerning the Ketogenic diet. These answers may help you to better clarify your ideas.

## What are the feelings in the first phase of this diet?

In most cases before starting this diet you were on an incorrect diet. In fact, your body was using glucose as its main source of energy. The moment you cut carbs drastically instead, your body suffers, so you may experience small feelings of stress or weakness, but after this first phase your metabolism will enjoy these changes. You then have to go through an initial normal period of adaptation. This is a temporary state, and the transition from one period to the next should be facilitated by some of your actions, such as keeping yourself constantly hydrated.

The moment you enter a state of ketosis, after a few days or weeks, you can begin to enjoy the benefits of the action of your metabolism.

## After how long does one adapt to the Ketogenic diet?

Not everyone can adapt best immediately to the Ketogenic diet. The adaptation process can take up to a maximum of 4 weeks, however, I can assure you that if you follow the directions in the food plan I mentioned, this process can be absolutely speeded up. In fact, there are even very tasty dishes in the food plan that will not make you regret the absence of carbohydrates and sugars from your diet.

Of course, your determination also plays a key role, because avoiding carbohydrates in the first few weeks can be a very tough challenge. If you also exercise, you can speed up this process, and your body will be forced to draw on your fat reserves.

## How can you tell if you are in a state of ketosis?

There are some signs that might let you know immediately that you are in a state of ketosis. Your breath can be a very important indicator, in fact if you wake up in the morning and feel a fruity taste in your mouth, your body is probably producing ketones. Your mental clarity may also be higher in this psychophysical state.

## Should calories be restricted?

As with all diets, you should not overconsume calories. For this diet, however, if followed correctly, calorie counting is not essential and indeed foods can be consumed until full. This happens because the diet does not promote weight gain and lowers the levels of insulin that is the hormone that stores fat.

## Is there a risk of leaving the state of ketosis?

Getting out of the state of ketosis is very simple, we need to clarify this point. When you consume a meal with even medium to small amounts of carbohydrates you can get out of the state of ketosis, but this condition actually lasts only a few hours. Your body always prefers to consume glucose if it is available. However, there are some actions that could help you preserve the state of ketosis such as periods of fasting or the consumption of certain types of fats, known as MCTs.

## Does this diet help weight loss and improve blood sugar levels?

Yes this diet is very popular not only because it allows you to lose weight but also because it lowers the glucose levels in your blood. If you take some particular medications that affect your blood glucose levels, you should talk to your doctor before following this diet.

## Can athletes follow this diet?

The answer to this question is obviously yes. All people who have an active lifestyle can follow this dietary regimen, which is also well compatible with those who consume a lot of energy during the day. In fact, ketones allow athletes to improve their performance. If your workout, however, is very intense, it is advisable to consume a small amount of energy-giving carbohydrates before the start. At this stage you will get out of the state of ketosis however you will only get back into it after a few hours.

# What is the difference between the Low Carb diet and the Ketogenic diet?

Low-carb diets differ from ketogenic because the latter is somewhat more restrictive. On Low Carb diets as much as 150 grams of carbohydrates per day are consumed, whereas to enter a state of ketosis in most cases one cannot exceed 30-40 grams of carbohydrates per day. The Ketogenic diet is also much higher in fat than a Low Carb diet and is also low in protein.

# Conclusions

We have come to the conclusion of this book. Right now you might be thinking that you are at the end of the journey you embarked on by starting to read this book, I don't want it to be that way. This book should be just the beginning for you, it should be the foundation on which your diet will rest and which you can rely on whenever you feel the need. You will never feel lost or alone if you read the advice I have given you, I can assure you that you will see results at a glance if you do as I have indicated. I can tell you for sure because I have experienced this firsthand and I can assure you that I have alternated between good diets but never achieved results like these. If you are tired of the usual routine and want to get rid of those extra pounds once and for all, this is the book for you. Don't look for other books on other diets, don't procrastinate on starting this new experience, you absolutely must take action.

This is a pivotal moment, this is the moment when you have to match theory with practice, don't make excuses, don't convince yourself that you have to wait for more time, that you are not ready yet, that you will never achieve these results by simply reading a book. That's just excuses, that's your old way of thinking resurfacing!

That's all you have to get rid of, you have to cleanse your mind and start thinking in a new, different way. I tell you this from the bottom of my heart, as if I were a friend to you, being comfortable with yourself is the greatest gift any person can give themselves. Waking up and having the courage to look in the mirror, to weigh yourself, to be proud of the achievements you have made is very nice. You cannot deprive yourself of these satisfactions just because you have low self-esteem or even worse out of laziness.

Now you have really received all the theoretical knowledge about the Ketogenic diet and also the knowledge to put into practice, you also have at your disposal a detailed 21-day weekly plan and in addition you can follow the many tips and quick recipes I have provided to enrich your diet. As soon as you close this book I would like you to start right away by beginning to reorganize your refrigerator and pantry with the foods I have suggested here, it could be the beginning of a new path that can make you approach food differently.

It's just up to you to be able to create a healthy eating protocol that can align perfectly with your lifestyle.

What you have learned in this book you will have to put into practice. Don't be satisfied with the 3-week food plan of the Ketogenic diet I have given you but try to do more. Doing this diet is not just about losing a few pounds, yes that is important too, I know, but it is more importantly about revolutionizing your approach to food to have a healthier lifestyle. Remember that this is a diet that has beneficial effects for your whole body. Not only will you lose weight but you will also feel better about yourself and your body will benefit, you really have nothing to lose.

Yes, there will be difficult moments, where everything will seem to be too heavy, especially at first because of the initial lack of sugar you were used to, but you have the strength and are absolutely capable of overcoming them.

After the first phase there will be the descent phase, where it will be easier and more enjoyable to live with this new dietary regimen. Consider that you are giving yourself a gift to yourself because seeing and feeling finally fit in your body is the greatest gift any of us can give ourselves. Take a moment for yourself and your well-being. Start treating your body as it deserves, never forget that it is the one thing that will be with you forever, so treat it with care.

Rediscover the pleasure of eating your vegetables, fish, eggs or cheeses, and adapt your diet to your work perhaps by preparing one of the easy recipes I have shown you the night before, I can assure you that if you can do this you will feel much lighter, with lots of energy and more efficient.

I bet that at least once you happened to see people who despite doing hundreds of things were full of energy. Their secret is definitely nutrition; this is the only thing that differentiates us. If one man has more energy than another, it is simply because he has best understood how to nourish himself and puts it into practice in his life.

Now it's your turn, it's time to start your food revolution and start        birthing         your        new        self!

# Intermittent Fasting

The complete diet to lose weight fast and lose weight without hunger. Food plan and recipes included

CLAUDIA RODRIGUEZ

# Introduction

I have tried many diets during my life but surely the Intermittent Fasting diet is the one that had the most amazing results on my body, as I could see not only weight loss but also a significant increase in muscle mass. I actually discovered it almost by accident, it was summertime and I was lying on my lawn chair in my backyard, I wanted to get some sun that day, to fight boredom I decided to read a gossip magazine (something I usually did not do). However, I thought that in the summer I too had the right to relax and do some mundane activities.

As I was boredly flipping through the magazine, I saw an article that immediately caught my attention. It was about the well-known singer Beyoncé, it was said that she was following a diet that had not only made her lose several kilograms in a short time making her even more beautiful, but was also having a very positive impact on her health.

It was mentioned in the article that this diet was depopulating in America, where more and more celebrities were interested in this new way of eating. What was even more curious was that the doctor creator of this diet was one of the world's greatest scholars-Dr. Walter Longo.

This reassured me because this diet did not come from some crazy idea of crazy people, but from years of research carried out by the most famous doctors in the world. I am not a nutritionist, however, I trust the opinion of those who have studied extensively in a particular field, in this case diets, and I myself have monitored them so much, and tried them directly on my own skin, that I have become a writer specializing in this subject.

The thing that made me think and passionate about it was that not only could this diet allow you to lose weight and slim down in a short time, but also drastically improve your health condition.

I then decided to adopt it and start practicing it, I had tried many of them over time, some of them even very good, so much so that I had already talked about them in several books I had written, such as the ketogenic diet and the sirt diet, so initially I was not very confident about undertaking a new one, totally unknown to me. The results, however, were not long in coming; I immediately noticed that not only was I losing weight quickly, but I was not even experiencing that unpleasant feeling of hunger.

My body was beginning to become just what I had always wanted, and those extra pounds I had accumulated over time, due to completely incorrect dietary regimens, had now become an old memory.

Contrary to what a person may think, a dietary regimen can also be adopted for life. This is clearly only in case it is healthy and makes you lose weight without worsening the condition of your body. Intermittent Fasting is a dietary regimen that falls precisely within these conditions. That is why I still apply intermittent fasting in my life at certain times.

I decided to write this book certainly not to showcase my achievements, but to share with you all that I have learned over time. Should you decide to follow my directions, always remember that I am a person who has tested on himself everything he communicates to you, and deepened everything with specific studies.

I would like this to be a manual for you, but also a real guide to follow even in the weeks after reading the book. That is why I decided to also include an eating plan inside, so you will have a good tool to follow in the coming days. You will certainly not feel lost and you will be able to take action right away.

In this diet regimen you do not consume products that are hard to find in supermarkets, for these very reasons it is not a difficult diet to follow. Nor will you have to spend hundreds of euros to buy special products, far from it.

You will simply have to learn to eat intelligently, alternating hours of fasting in your daily routine. I know this makes you think you will go terribly hungry, I thought so too, the reality however is quite different.

Intermittent Fasting is also famous in the world because according to many, the positive effects that are released in the body allow humans to extend their lives. In fact, you will probably realize that day by day you will have more and more energy and a different mental clarity. You will be more and more in focus and hardly experience unpleasant feelings of fatigue and stress.

Moreover, it is a diet that can be adopted by everyone, regardless of age or gender.

Obviously in case you suffer from particular diseases, as I always specify in each of my books, it would be advisable to consult your doctor before following any food diet.

Now then, all that remains is for me to wish you well in your reading and to step confidently into this new world.

I hope you can find all the information you need to make you understand every single aspect of this natural diet, which is effective for losing weight fast while also regaining health and well-being for your body.

# What is intermittent fasting and what are its benefits?

It may sound a bit strange, but deliberately restricting food consumption can be one of the most effective ways to keep your health in order. For example, as scientists have found, intermittent fasting is not only the most effective diet for losing weight, but also a great way to reduce the risk of many diseases (diabetes, cardiovascular problems, cancer).

This diet has become a viral trend in the United States. Its followers include Hugh Jackman, Tim Ferriss, and Beyoncé. In Silicon Valley, senior executives of large companies apply intermittent corporate fasting, follow diets with their employees. Many of them say intermittent fasting has helped them lose weight and gain more energy.

Intermittent fasting is a dietary pattern in which eating is only allowed at a certain time. For example, only 4 hours a day or 8 hours or 5 days a week. The rest of the time, you should forget about food, limiting yourself to drinking: water or (in mild variations of fasting) fruit and vegetable juices are allowed. The most popular model is the "5 by 2," which I will tell you about later.

One of the scientists working in the anti-aging field at the University of Southern California-Walter Longo, who wrote the book "The Longevity Diet," introducing his diet to the public says it improves health, prolongs life and at the same time allows people to enjoy a normal diet 25 days a month.

The 16/8 pattern involves 16 hours of fasting and 8 hours of non-fasting. For example, a person may eat between 10 a.m. and 6 p.m., eating 3-4 meals during this period. The rest of the time the person should restrict himself to consuming only drinks.

The 14/10 scheme is one of the most beneficial options, here you alternate 14 hours of fasting with 10 hours in which you can eat anything. Such a regimen is affordable for almost everyone, because in a nutshell it means something like: you can eat whatever you want from 10:00 to 20:00, so almost the whole day, then leaving the fasting hours for the late evening until the next morning. Of course, then we will see in more detail what is recommended to eat and what is not.

The most popular pattern, however, is 5/2. It consists of eating 5 days a week and fasting on 2. Also, fasting for 2 days does not mean a complete rejection of food, but limiting the calorie content to 1/4 the usual amount (so about 600 calories for men, 500 for women). On fasting days both men and women should drink plenty of water, and in some cases drinks such as tea are also recommended.

Intermittent fasting is based on the basic principle of metabolism.

There are two main energy reserves in our bodies, which are formed from the excess calories consumed during the day: fat and glycogen.

Whatever we do, physical movement of any kind requires the expenditure of energy; even a state of rest, when we are immobile, is an apparent rest, because while the body is living, processes are constantly taking place within it that require energy replenishment.

Thus, there are internal metabolism mechanisms in our bodies: each cell requires a constant flow of energy to continue living. In practice, however, none of us during the day empties all our glycogen stores to start burning fat and producing energy, because we are constantly eating something from the moment we get up until we sleep. Therefore, this way of eating does not allow us to lose weight. At this rate, the body itself seems to get used to burning sugar first and not fat.

The most obvious effect of fasting days in this format is weight loss. Because of the rather long fasting intervals, the body receives fewer calories, which quickly affects body volume.

For these very reasons, this diet had excellent effects on my body, and it allowed me to lose several kilograms in a very short time.

In addition, according to Walter Longo's studies, Intermittent Fasting reduces the risk of type II diabetes.

When we apply this dietary regimen, the body's sensitivity to insulin increases, which causes a decrease in the level of this hormone in the blood. And a low insulin level forces the body to actively transform existing fat stores into energy.

It also has effects on slowing cellular aging. In fact, intermittent fasting increases the body's resistance to oxidative stress, one of the main causes of aging and chronic diseases. According to experiments performed over time, animals, getting 20 percent less than their normal caloric intake, lived longer than humans. Now of course in most cases humans live longer than animals, but the way of life has profoundly changed with the evolution of the human species.

This diet also serves to improve heart health. Intermittent fasting reduces the effects of a number of risk factors that can adversely affect the cardiovascular system. Through it, blood pressure is normalized and the overall condition of the heart and blood vessels improves.

Another aspect to consider is that intermittent fasting inhibits the growth of cancer cells and at the same time increases the effectiveness of chemotherapy, which means that it increases the chances of winning the fight against cancer. Of course, by this we certainly do not want to tell people with cancer to change their diet to cure themselves, but simply that this combined with chemotherapy can bring benefits. In all cases if one is in such a delicate condition one should consult one's doctor and follow the advice of experts.

During the intermittent fasting period also I felt much more focused and my brain worked clearly and sharply.

Many scholars assume that intermittent fasting may become one of the methods to prevent all kinds of brain disorders, including depression.

In fact, you should know that fasting increases the ability of cells to resist stress (similar to exercise).

Intermittent Fasting has been very successful among American celebrities first and then the rest of the world partly because it eliminates the desire to eat sweets and junk food, accustoming the body to effectively burn fat; modern science also confirms many other health benefits.

For example, a study presented in 2011 at a scientific conference at the American College of Cardiology showed that fasting stimulates a huge increase in growth hormone: 1300% in women and 2000% in men! Growth hormone is sometimes called fitness hormone because it plays an important role in muscle growth and weight loss. To enhance these effects, bodybuilders often administer it by injection.

Contrary to what many people believe, it is also suitable for athletes.

Strength training on an empty stomach and at a low blood sugar level leads to increased production of growth hormone, which has a positive effect on both muscle strength and fat loss, since any training under conditions of energy deprivation requires the body to extract this energy from internal reserves and, in particular, fat stores.

The body gradually learns to work not only on simple fuels (glucose from sugars and carbohydrates), but also on free fatty acids.

I have tried this kind of training on myself as well, finding the benefits, although clearly it is something that needs to be done gradually, so that the body gets used to adapting to it slowly over time.

# The Intermittent Fasting "5/2"

The essence of the 5: 2 diet is simple. Five days a week you can eat as much as you want, and in two days you will have to practice fasting. This type of fasting is also known as the Fast Diet because it allows you to lose weight in a very short time. In this case, you do not have to eat only small salads or make huge sacrifices.

You can choose, on the lighter days, the dishes you want to eat, the important thing is that the daily calorie intake should not be more than 500 kcal for women and not more than 600 kcal for men. Another mandatory rule regarding "low calorie" days, these should not be consecutive, you should arrange them on two separate days of the week, for example, Tuesday and Friday. Practicing fasting for two consecutive days could be dangerous and certainly not advisable.

Such "intermittent fasting," according to Mosley, could provide a powerful jolt to the body, which will not only force intensive use of old fat stores, but also initiate processes that will bring great benefits.

Everyone knows: when you take a good shower, you feel like you've been reborn. This is not really a metaphor. Exposure to high temperatures is a kind of stress for cells, forcing them to actively renew themselves, look for damaged ones and restore them. A similar process that forces the body to use its hidden reserves is triggered by short-term fasting.

Only during fasting do the processes go deeper, down to the regulation of the hypothalamus, the part of the brain responsible for, among other things, hunger and metabolism (metabolic processes). In the absence of calories, the body signals the brain to slow down the metabolism and prolong the pleasure of eating.

The slower the metabolism, the longer we can live. In addition, low metabolism reduces the number of free radicals, which play one of the most important roles in the development of disease and aging.

Actually, according to one of the theories of aging it is about the difficulty for our bodies to fight free radicals that eventually take over.

# The main thing is to alternate

So maybe for the sake of youth it is worth limiting ourselves to food several days a week, and not just two?

"The focus of this diet is precisely in the alternation of good nutrition and fasting," says Andrei Garazha, an expert in applied biomedical technologies and life extension research. - In principle, any abrupt change in diet takes a person out of the comfort zone, forcing the body to strain, to work in an advanced mode to balance all the changes. In addition, such fluctuations allow one to adjust one's optimal balance of fats, proteins and carbohydrates for a given person. If you fast too long, there are many negative effects: reproductive function begins to experience problems as well as your digestive system and exacerbation of chronic diseases.

So forget about fasting for more days than you should during the week, you will only hurt yourself. I can assure you from my own experience that if you alternate days of dieting with days of good nutrition, you will not suffer from hunger and most importantly you will immediately feel much fitter.

Most of us are used to eating three times a day and having a delicious and satisfying snack between meals. Scientists have calculated that while in the 1970s the break between meals was nearly 5 hours, today it is only 3.5. That is, we eat as regularly as children do. But the child needs this for development, while the adult "gains" in this way more and more extra pounds.

Many people cannot afford to give up snacks or even reduce portions. Planning a day of fasting is not something always looked upon favorably by the society in which we live. Instead, the diet simply suggests regular food "dumping" days.

*"Fasting days are a great opportunity to get rid of stocks,"* says nutritionist Micaela Pudicini.

Every one of us has happened to make several attempts to lose weight, and when we tried, our bodies began to cry out for revenge. Many times this happens when we adopt drastic diets that put our bodies under great stress. At the end of the diet we will not only eat the same amount of food as before it, but frustration will lead us to consume even much more.

If you apply the intermittent fasting diet, your body will get used to periodic restrictions and tolerate them more easily.

Nutritionists are also confident of the benefits of fasting days. The body maximizes resources for muscle recovery on the fasting day following the two days when we feed normally. If we reduce the amount of calories on the fasting day, it is possible to achieve significant fat burning.

However, Michael Mosley one of the creators of the intermittent fasting methodology stresses the importance of not gorging on days when one can eat normally. In fact, it would be advisable to eat "within reasonable limits." Some nutritionists are even harsher and argue that it is necessary to eat moderately on "loading" days. To make you better understand what is meant, you should know that on average a man who leads a sedentary life and is therefore not very physically active will have to consume about 1800 Kcal while a woman in the same condition about 1500 Kcal. This difference in calories is due to the slimmer body of women compared to that of men.

It is important before starting the fasting period to first determine how many calories are taken in daily. After all, the limit of 500-600 kcal is a very low figure but one that allows one to avoid starvation.

To begin with, on days considered fasting days you can try reducing the calorie content you consume daily, by one-third and see your body's response. If your body responds well and you don't feel destroyed, you can probably follow this type of diet without any problems.

## What to eat to lose weight

What to eat during fasting days? Can I eat anything within 500-600 Kcal?

These were the questions I initially asked myself to which I later found answers that I would like to share with you.

500-600 Kcal can be absorbed in different ways by different products. For example, 500 calories may be present in a hamburger with fries or in two large cups of latte with cereal.

But how much benefit will we get if we eat a series of chops and then starve for the rest of the day? So in order not to stress your body on the fasting day and not overeat the next day, you should carefully consider the menu.

Author of the "5: 2" diet, Dr. Michael Mosley recommends giving preference to **protein-rich** foods-they are more satiating. Eating exclusively protein food is not always good, however; in fact, using only protein may not have the best effect on the kidneys.

Therefore, you should include low glycemic index carbohydrates in your diet. A combination of these foods works best to reduce hunger. For example, you could eat turkey with brown rice, chicken breast with brown bread, oatmeal for breakfast, and fish for lunch. There are many options you can choose to unleash your imagination. The important thing is not to resort to quick carbohydrate snacks (baked goods with white flour, cakes with cream and fried fast food).

Of course, at first it will be hard to resist the desire not to eat something, but gradually you will get used to it. Next I will show you a number of tasty recipes you can prepare and also an eating plan you can follow in the 4 weeks following the diet.

"We often don't eat because we are hungry," says Michael Mauchly. - We eat when we are bored, when we are thirsty, when food is nearby or only at lunchtime. The human brain artfully convinces us that we are hungry, in almost any situation. But often these are just learned reactions from external stimuli. Yes, on a fasting day you should certainly try to focus on something other than food, entertain yourself by doing your own thing, and be distracted from thinking about hunger, so that at least at first you can get used to this new mode. Even if you yourself do not notice it, your brain will gradually be reprogrammed, and the feeling of hunger will slowly disappear.

# Intermittent Fasting 16/8

Another type of Intermittent Fasting is what is known with 16/8, that is, 16 hours of fasting and 8 in which you can eat.

Before I explain in detail how intermittent fasting 16/8 works and thus how it differs from what I explained in the last chapter, I want to tell you that these are alternative forms of intermittent fasting from which you can choose. Whichever choice you make you can achieve the same results. I want to explain them all to you so that you can consciously choose the one that best fits your life, and therefore also your needs.

The rules of the 16/8 diet involve no breakfast, a large lunch, an afternoon snack and an early dinner -- in fact, food is only allowed from noon to 8 p.m. or 10 a.m. to 6 p.m. depending on how you want to set it up according to your daily rhythm. The advantage of intermittent fasting is the normalization of metabolism. This diet is especially popular with us women, in fact, there are a great many who adopt it in the world, however, men can also get the same benefits.

The 16/8 diet is a dietary system of fasting for 16 hours a day. Since most of this time is spent in the evening and night hours, thus of rest and sleep, such a diet is quite easy to follow. Moreover, although a reduction in caloric intake is desirable, it is not necessary. As mentioned above in all cases it is preferable to avoid eating too much food in excess, because then you can see the results only after a long time.

Always try to follow a healthy eating regimen, without overdoing it but also not going hungry. You should never stress your body or bring it into an uncomfortable condition.

With intermittent fasting 16/8, one specifically seeks to lower glucose levels and improve insulin production processes. The 16/8 diet can also optimize the production of the hunger hormone: leptin.

# How does it work?

Eating carbohydrate foods leads to increased blood glucose levels. If there is too much energy from this glucose, it is sent to fat stores. Avoiding carbohydrates or eating them in small amounts lowers glucose levels, thereby forcing the body to use up reserves-this is the principle behind the work of the no-carb keto diet.

First of all, the 16/8 diet helps fight insulin resistance syndrome and related diseases such as obesity and hypertension.

In addition, the hormonal changes mentioned above are of particular importance: low insulin and high growth hormone cause the release of the powerful fat-burning hormone, namely norepinephrine, into the bloodstream. On average, intermittent fasting increases metabolic rate by 3.6 to 14 percent.

Intermittent fasting and the 16/8 diet can be seen as an effective way to combat sugar addiction. Often, the feeling of hunger is not real hunger at all, but only a signal from the body that indicates the presence of low blood glucose levels.

Many people believe that after a few hours that you fast immediately you may feel hungry, in fact this is not the case, in fact if you experience a feeling of hunger this will come from other stimuli that your body makes you relate back to those of hunger. In fact it usually takes 30 to 40 hours of fasting to activate the actual hunger mechanisms, these are characterized by a sharp increase in the stress hormone and the hunger hormone i.e. leptin, which will make you think exclusively about food.

In other words, intermittent fasting optimizes your metabolism without triggering the negative processes associated with complete refusal to eat.

Initially, the intermittent fasting system and the 16/8 diet were used by athletes as a way to increase lean muscle mass without fat.

In the case of using the 16/8 diet to lose weight, you should perform a low-intensity, long-duration fat-burning workout in the morning. You could, for example, pedal at a slow pace on an exercise bike or take a brisk walk or even do the activities I will point out in the appropriate chapter.

I have long since decided to train on an empty stomach at low intensity. Not only do I feel better about myself but the results are also much more noticeable. I have never experienced any problems with strength or even energy drops. You could of worked out during the morning if you want to do it during the fasting period, maybe as soon as you wake up so you have enough energy to get through the day as best you can.

Intermittent fasting changes the way metabolism works: instead of processing food, the body switches to using existing reserves. As a result, hormone levels change and cells begin to get rid of accumulated "debris": this process is called autophagy.

Studies show that with intermittent fasting, the level of production of growth hormone (remember it is responsible for increasing muscle mass and burning fat) increases by about 5 times. At the same time, insulin levels decrease, helping the body quickly extract energy from fat stores.

On a 16/8 diet, the most effective time to exercise is in the morning, when blood sugar is at its lowest. Note that the first few workouts on an empty stomach, as I anticipated earlier, can seem quite difficult (especially for people who are not in shape), but if you have the perseverance to start accustoming your body gradually, you will see that your body will adapt and you can start to experience the benefits.

# Warrior's Diet - Intermittent Fasting

The so-called Warrior's Diet is a variation of the diets seen above, and it helps to lose extra pounds in no time, improve concentration and increase energy levels.

Quarantine and Covid-19 have changed our habits and also our schedules. Many people wake up near lunchtime or even sleep during the day to wake up later in the evening, so that evening meals have become the main meals during the day for many.

But even this nuance can be turned to your advantage. One diet that is spreading very fast, especially in the West is the "warrior diet," which provides a powerful fat-burning effect precisely because of night eating.

In short, its essence is simple: be abstinent during the day and eat as much as you want before going to bed.

This is the method of nutritionist Auryu Hofmclair, a well-known author in the health and fitness world. It is based on the diet of ancient warriors who ate sparsely during the day and then feasted at night.

People on diets are advised to eat 85 to 90 percent of their daily calories overnight. That can reach an accumulation of 1800 kcal per meal for a woman or up to 2700 calories for a man.

This way of eating is not revolutionary for humanity.

Moreover, it has a rich and complex history. Presumably, the earliest records of the Warrior diet date back to ancient Greece: then this method was praised by Pythagoras; its advocates were also Hippocrates and later Paracelsus.

If you look closely, elements of such a diet in the form of fasting can be found in almost every religion in the world. Judaism recognizes several days of abstinence from food throughout the year, Muslims fast during the holy month of Ramadan, and Christians observe 40-day dietary restrictions during Lent.

In today's wellness world, so-called intermittent fasting is often referred to as a method of purifying and rebooting the body as well as increasing its performance. Most importantly, from an aesthetic point of view, it effectively helps to reduce weight and improve the "quality" of the body. The scientific community, as mentioned above, also supports intermittent fasting, emphasizing its benefits for the health of the heart, brain and other organs. However, experts do not recommend such a nutritional system for athletes and pregnant women!

To be precise, the intermittent fasting warrior diet did not appear very long ago. Oryu Hofmkler developed it in 2001 after years of monitoring the health and fitness of his Israeli special forces colleagues.

It helped the author to be as efficient as possible during military service. But lately the diet has gained popularity and has been heralded as an innovation. Most likely, this is related to our common fear of losing fitness by self-isolation and changing habits.

# How does the warrior diet work?

The diet includes 20 hours of fasting (or very limited food intake) and a four-hour evening window during which you can eat as much as you want and almost anything you want.

After all, there were no forbidden foods in the soldiers' diet. Of course, nutrient-rich foods and lots of fruits, vegetables and protein are encouraged. But if you are attracted to pizza some night, why not? The important thing is not to go over what is allowed (85-90% of daily calories).

If calorie counting is not your thing, then it is best to strictly follow Hofmeckler's rules. The scholar recommends making your evening dinner from healthy fats and large portions of protein, particularly sources such as chicken or lean meats, cheese, yogurt and other dairy products.

In addition, the author strongly advises not to neglect exercise. With this diet you will still have enough energy to use for exercise.

## What you can eat in any quantity

There is no need to count calories if you eat Hofmeckler-approved foods in the evening.

-Fruits and vegetables: try to eat different kinds of fruits and vegetables every day. Vegetables of all groups are recommended: dark green, red and orange, legumes (beans and peas), starchy and others.

-Cereals: whole grain bread, pasta; quinoa, brown rice, bulgur and oats.

-Dairy products: cheese, yogurt, whole milk.

-Proteins: chicken, turkey, lean meats, seafood, hard-boiled eggs, nuts, soy products. Never give up protein-a warrior needs it to maintain and build muscle mass.

-Drinks: during the day, you can drink as many low-calorie drinks as you want (tea, coffee, clean drinking water, vegetable juices). In the evening -as much as you want, including wine.

## What is best to avoid

I repeat, just as in the other types of intermittent fasting there are no foods that are completely forbidden on the "warrior" diet, but even on this diet it is better for some not to abuse them. These are for example:

-Sweets and refined sugar: eat fewer cookies and candy bars. Imagine you are like a warrior in the countryside, isolated from the world, you will need other foods rather than these to survive.

-Salty snacks (chips, bread croutons, etc.): for something crunchy and tasty, try vegetables with hummus or guacamole.

-Sugar drinks. Try to limit intake of soda, energy drinks with added sugar

## How to deal with the day?

Yes, I know you are now asking yourself, how do I survive the other 20 hours of the day? That's a good question, I asked myself that question too before I tried this dietary regimen, which I must say is definitely not very suitable for my lifestyle, but which for a short time I wanted to try, so that I could then write about it with more mastery.

In fact certainly intermittent fasting set up in this way is not very easy to follow.

During the day, you can quell your appetite by drinking plenty of water, but also various beverages such as tea or coffee or vitamin water without sugar.

Should you compulsorily eat in the night hours? Actually, you don't always need to wait until the evening!

Choose your window at any time of the day, depending on the time of day that suits you best. You can go on a 4-hour fast in the morning, for example, and during the remaining 20 hours, as they say, tighten your belt. However, most people who practice this fasting mode postpone the time frame until the evening.

## Pros and cons of the warrior diet

As with all diets, the Hofmeckler method has advantages and disadvantages.

Pros of the diet:

It really helps to reduce weight (up to 9 kilograms per month).

Reduces blood sugar levels: during hungry hours, insulin levels decrease and fat cells release stored sugar to be used as energy.

It fights inflammation in the body (a consequence of the

previous point).

It reduces the risk of cardiovascular disease.

It improves memory and the ability to think clearly.

Diet cons:

It is certainly quite difficult to follow. Although our ancestors could easily live 20 hours without food, this is not the norm in modern society.

It can also lead to overeating during the hours when you are allowed to do so. In fact, it is possible that during happy hours you will eat too much because of the concession of being allowed to do so, and not at all in the healthy way you should. So you have to pay close attention to this aspect.

It is also not suitable for certain types of people (pregnant or lactating women, athletes).

It can lead to possible nutrient deficiency (which is resolved by taking vitamin and mineral complexes).

My advice is, if you want to try this type of intermittent fasting, to apply the warrior diet only for limited periods of time and especially after you have already practiced other types of intermittent fasting, such as the ones I have mentioned in the past chapters.

After the period when you decide to follow this style of eating, you should adopt similar diets, such as 5/2 fasting or 16/8 fasting, before returning to a normal diet, so that the return to normal food intake is more gradual.

# OMAD diet: once a day

We have arrived at what is considered by many to be the most extreme version of intermittent fasting. It is not recommended to start directly from this type of diet, but I suggest you always do a gradual process. I only applied it to try it, as I did the warrior one described in the previous chapter, for a small period of time, and I don't think you should apply it for long periods of time either, because it may become unsustainable. I will explain what it is so that you can better understand what I really mean by these words.

In a nutshell, the "one-time" diet called OMAD, which is an acronym in English for "one meal a day" consists of the fact that a person can eat anything, but only once, during the 24 hours. The dish can be a double cheeseburger for example, but also a bowl of ice cream or a healthy and nutritious dish, which is what is most strongly recommended and what I have taken on myself in my short trial period, you can really eat what you want, and especially in the quantities you want.

The idea is that by limiting your calorie intake during the day, you can have a great meal once a day and still lose weight. You can keep drinking water and unsweetened coffee and tea, but eating everything else is forbidden for the rest of the day.

The once-a-day diet is a time-limited intermittent fast, in which people on the diet eat nothing for 23 hours. Most people who practice it do it at night, skipping breakfast and enjoying the meal in the middle of the day, and during the rest of the day hours they can think about what they will eat the next day. As you can therefore understand, it can be really difficult to follow such a dietary regimen.

The "one-time" diet is so extreme that other versions of fasting seem almost trivial, such as the 16/8 diet compared to this one.

When you eat only once a day, you are probably consuming far fewer calories than usual. As a result, your weight will tend to drop.

When you practice a "one-time" diet, it is very easy to feel unfit to do it, and to give up quickly. I understand you, however, I can tell you that if you were comfortable with the other types of intermittent fasting, you could try it without any problem, because I did it myself, only to come to the conclusion that it was too extreme for me, and much prefer the lighter forms of intermittent fasting described in the previous chapters.

Long periods of fasting often generate cyclical changes in weight, hormones and metabolism. So that's why in case you decide to try it, I recommend adopting it only for a few days during the year.

## Is the OMAD diet harmful to health?

The idea behind fasting is that it gives your vital organs, digestive hormones and metabolic functions a break and reduces oxidative stress in your body. It is believed to improve body tissue function, reduce inflammation, and reduce the risk of chronic disease and diabetes. I have told you about this in depth in the other chapters as well.

Surely with this extreme diet you have results, so you'll see right away your weight drop dramatically, for these very reasons I don't recommend making it a diet regimen to be followed constantly over time, it should be as a quick means to make you lose weight faster at certain times of the year, a real boost to your diet, an accelerator.

You must also consider that there are some major risks, and potential adverse effects associated with this diet:

- Overeating: when you only have an hour to eat, you may eat a lot of food at once, and in the long run stop responding to your body's signals that you are full or hungry.
- Lack of nutrients: without fruits, vegetables, salads and dairy products, your body may lack healthy ingredients and vitamins. Also consider this when you choose to eat a fatty hamburger rather than a tomato and cucumber salad.

Surely you must also consider that it will be very difficult, with such a dietary regimen, to exercise regularly.

If you still want to try the OMAD diet, take in a wide variety of nutrient-rich foods such as fruits, vegetables, whole grains and lean proteins. Do not go on a "one-time" diet if you are pregnant, breastfeeding or taking medications that require nutrients to have effects.

Although there are no short-term side effects, researchers have yet to understand how extreme fasting might affect a person in the long term.

Try to get more sleep at night and thus get sufficient rest.

Following these rules will enable the body to remain healthy.

# For whom is Intermittent Fasting not indicated? Answer to the most common questions

As with any food system, there are pros and cons. If you live with any of the following conditions, you should not follow this dietary regimen:

- If you suffer from immune diseases;
- In cases of impaired liver and kidney function;
- With the presence of various diseases of the gastrointestinal tract such as gastritis that can bring severe stomach pain;
- When leading a very active lifestyle;
- In a state of high stress, as well as if you suffer from neurosis or insomnia;
- You are a pregnant or lactating woman.

Also, you should not start intermittent fasting if you are sick or simply not feeling well. You can practice this technique only if you are absolutely healthy.

In any case, before making such an important decision, be sure to always consult your doctor to eliminate any possible risk.

I have collected a series of questions in this chapter that may clarify your thoughts and doubts about this type of diet.

**Question number 1)**

## Is intermittent fasting preferable or following a type of diet with fractionated meals throughout the day?

This is very subjective, but it should be said up front that intermittent fasting is not suitable for people who need to eat often and in small portions. You could try interspersing perhaps a short period of intermittent fasting with a ketogenic diet, so as to give you an increase in weight loss during the period when you practice fasting, and then maintain the weight and go down again by practicing the ketogenic diet, a very simple diet to follow, just on this topic if you may be interested, I have written a very simple and well done book, entitled precisely Ketogenic Diet.

## Question number 2)

## Is it possible to drink coffee during intermittent fasting?

Yes, in this type of diet, it is not only possible but also necessary to drink coffee to suppress the feeling of hunger. The only advice is to drink it bitter, without adding sugar, but even with regard to this, I again emphasize not to overdo it, however, with the quantities, perhaps replacing coffee with green tea or black tea, and in case you suffer from gastritis or colitis I would really advise to avoid abusing it, and not to practice the intense fasting types.

## Question number 3)

## How much weight can you lose with intermittent fasting?

As a rule, when you are very overweight, the weight disappears faster, and very often overweight people lose up to

7-10 kg in the first month of this regimen. However, everything here is very individual and to be tested on your own skin. You may lose only a few kg as well as several kg.

**Question number 4)**

**Can you exercise during Intermittent Fasting?**

You can train during intermittent fasting, the important thing is to balance your diet properly on these days. Protein and slow carbohydrates are a must on these days. It is also very important to choose the right time to train. To choose the right time you should mind your physical condition and focus on your well-being.

**Question #5)**

**Is intermittent fasting also practiced by bodybuilders?**

This method is actually practiced in bodybuilding as well, especially during the drying period (before a competition). It is best in any case to do your workout on an empty stomach on those days, to burn as many calories as possible. Also, it is best to consume maximum calories after training.

# Intermittent Fasting Food Plan 16/8 and 5/2

In this part of the book I have decided to show you the food plan to follow should you wish to adopt Intermittent Fasting 16/8. Of course you can decide to follow it to the letter or make variations. You can follow this food plan for the first 4 weeks and evaluate whether or not you were satisfied with it. In case this has given you satisfaction, you may continue or replace some of these meals with others you prefer.

## Monday

For breakfast you can drink green tea, herbal tea or bitter coffee, in all cases you should not use sugar in any drink. You can also drink plenty of water, this is advisable at any time of the day. Regarding breakfast in this eating plan I will always give you the same advice, simply because you cannot consume food since you are still in the 16 hours of fasting. However, in order not to suffer too much from the feeling of hunger, and get in shape for lunchtime, drinking something can distract you from this unpleasant feeling.

As for lunch (from 12 o'clock onwards) I recommend that you prepare a pasta with pesto, as a second course some vegetables and a spoonful of oil, and finish it all off with a piece of fruit. Remember that from this hour until the next 8 hours you can consume food.

For a snack at 4 p.m. you can have a fruit.

In the evening for dinner (remember to stay within 8 hours), you can have baked cod, rye bread and mixed vegetables. You can also accompany it with a small glass of wine.

## Tuesday

Tuesday's breakfast is always the same as Monday's. You can vary on things to drink but it is essential that there is no sugar.

For lunch you can have pasta with sauce and a salad with cherry tomatoes for a second course.

For snack you can have a small sandwich with cold cuts, avoid bologna or salami.

Instead, in the evening you could eat chicken breast with potatoes and vegetables.

## Wednesday

Breakfast identical to previous days, remember to always drink plenty to keep your body hydrated but absolutely avoid sugar consumption.

At lunchtime this time you can eat rice with a legume of your choice (peas, chickpeas, beans and so on). Finish your lunch with a good fruit.

In the afternoon you can eat some dried fruit.

Instead, in the evening he prepares a good baked chicken with potatoes.

## Thursday

Breakfast identical to previous days.

In lunch prepare a good vegetable couscous with a pinch of salt.

For snack a good fruit.

In the evening you can eat a sea bream with salad as a side dish, you can add a dash of oil and vinegar to season it.

## Friday

Breakfast identical to previous days.

For lunch you can make a pasta dish with zucchini and eat a chicken breast for a second course.

For snack, eat some dried fruit.

In the evening for dinner, prepare a slice of pork with vegetables and a drop of oil.

## Saturday

Breakfast identical to previous days.

For lunch you can have pasta with potatoes and sauce and for second course a salad with cherry tomatoes.

In the afternoon, one low-fat yogurt.

In the evening a pizza or otherwise any 8eating of your choice.

## Sunday

Breakfast identical to previous days.

For lunch, pasta with meat sauce. For second course a meat

roll.

For snack, a small bresaola sandwich.

In the evening you can have baked eggplant and a chicken breast.

You can also apply this eating plan in all subsequent weeks. You can vary the pasta dishes during lunch times or reverse some evenings with another. Basically, however, you should always eat healthfully. As you can see there are no sweets, chocolates or other high-sugar foods in the plan.

You can also apply this diet regimen to the 5/2 diet only in the latter case you should choose two days during the week on which to fast. Remember that these do not have to be consecutive and I recommend that you avoid choosing Saturdays and Sundays. It could become very tiring, especially if you live with other people to see them eating goodies over the weekend and fasting.

You could choose for fasting two days such as Monday and Thursday, because as I advised you in the specific chapter, it would be preferable for the two fasting days not to be consecutive, or Tuesday and Friday, you have in any case ample choice to test on your skin and try what remains most comfortable for you, based also on your daily routine.

# Mimic Fasting Diet

The Mima Fasting Diet is a relatively new diet that restricts calories only for a specific period of time. So it is likened to a type of intermittent fasting. It was also developed by Dr. Walter Longo, the Italian biologist and researcher I have already told you about.

Dr. Longo studied the effects of fasting on the body and tried to increase its positive effects without adopting fasting for too long. As a result of his research, Longo found a new way of nutrition: he created a diet that mimics only prolonged fasting, but at the same time does not deprive the body of so many calories for so long.

At the heart of the Mima Fasting diet are the ProLon (Dr. Walter Longo's company) five-day food plans prepared in advance once a month. That is, you don't need to eat this way for the whole month. Just once a month for five days. All meals and snacks are prepared with organic plant-based products that have undergone minimal processing.

The kits contain a small amount of protein and carbohydrates and lots of fats such as olives or flaxseed oil. You cannot eat anything else during these five days.

The first day of the diet provides about 1,090 calories (10 percent protein, 56 percent fat, 34 percent carbohydrates), while days 2 to 5 provide only 725 calories (9 percent protein, 44 percent fat, 47 percent carbohydrates).

This low-calorie, low-carbohydrate, low-fat diet forces the

body to produce energy from sources other than carbohydrates after glycogen stores are depleted. This process is called gluconeogenesis (not to be confused with ketosis).

Gluconeogenesis is a metabolic pathway that leads to the formation of glucose from noncarbohydrate compounds (specifically, pyruvate). Together with glycogenolysis, this pathway maintains the level of glucose in the blood, which is necessary for the functioning of many tissues and organs, mainly nerve tissue and erythrocytes.

According to one study, such a diet covers 34-54% of calories taken in normal daily diets. This calorie restriction leads to a physiological response involving: cell regeneration, reduced inflammation and fat loss.

Even before you decide to follow such a diet, you should absolutely always consult a nutritionist or gastroenterologist.

Thus, the purpose of the diet is to make your body think you are fasting while still providing the energy it needs to function. Let us warn you now: you will constantly experience a slight feeling of hunger.

Your five-day menu might look something like this.

# Day 1.

Breakfast: avocado, cucumber and mint salad.

Lunch: carrot soup with walnuts.

Dinner: avocado soup.

# Day 2.

Breakfast: Chia seed pudding and fresh or frozen berries in coconut milk.

Lunch: arugula and pomegranate salad.

Snack: a smoothie made with orange juice, olive oil and plum (apple) vinegar.

Dinner: zucchini noodles with stewed vegetables.

# Day #3.

Breakfast: spicy banana and cocoa pancakes.

Lunch: tapenade, that is, a puree, of olives with fresh vegetables.

# Day #4.

Breakfast: pear, arugula and almond salad.

Lunch: cauliflower soup with curry.

# Day #5.

Breakfast: flourless pumpkin muffins.

Lunch: vegetable salad with vinegar dressing.

Of course, you can choose your dishes as you like, just remember that they should all be vegetarian and you have to count the number of calories: the first day - 1090 kcal, the other four days - 725 kcal. Since it is also desirable to observe the balance of protein-fat-carbohydrates, clearly although I mention here this type of mimic fasting diet, for the sake of greater completeness of the text, this is definitely not a very easy diet to follow on your own, as it involves specific meals and weighed and targeted foods, so should you want to undertake it, it would be best to seek help from a nutritionist. He or she will be able to put together the optimal menu for you and calculate all the indicators.

For greater convenience, should you want to follow everything that is indicated by Dr. Walter Longo and this diet of his, you would necessarily have to buy his packages on the ProLon website, which cost an average of €199, which is also why therefore not being accessible to everyone, the high costs could be one of the major disadvantages of this dietary regimen.

# Common Mistakes Intermittent Fasting

When we decide to follow such a dietary regimen, so different from any other, it is easy to make mistakes without our realizing it. The first of these could be to accidentally raise insulin levels. Whenever you take in food that will activate your body's metabolic response, it will mean that you have broken the fast.

Common mistakes involve the intake of these foods that should instead be avoided during fasting hours:

-   Coffee creamer;
-   Almond milk;
-   Accidental ingestion of toothpaste or mouthwash;
-   Painkillers that contain sugar.

Whenever a person ingests any of these foods during the fasting hours, all he does is disrupt the processes that are activated in his body.

The second mistake concerns water intake, which is often insufficient. Fasting without enough water can be worse than not fasting. Damaged cells or other wastes in the body cannot be eliminated without being excreted.

In addition, your body does not consume the water you normally consume by eating food. If you are not properly hydrated, you are more likely to have headaches, muscle cramps and intense hunger.

If you want to eliminate toxins while fasting, it is important to drink, so I recommend following these tips:

- Plenty of water;
- 1-2 tablespoons of apple cider vinegar (suppresses hunger and promotes deeper fasting);
- Black, herbal or green tea;
- Black coffee.

The longer you fast, the more benefit you get from not taking food.

When you resume eating be very careful about your stomach. It contracts when you are hungry and its lining is thin, so overpowering it with food is not always a good idea.

Another mistake many people make is to avoid doing exercises while fasting. Even if your workout seems hard, you will benefit tremendously from fasting workouts.

Exercising on an empty stomach burns more fat because your body has nothing to digest right away. The body then pays attention to metabolic needs, and research shows that the first thing it targets is fat.

Also, you don't have to eat right after your workout. So if you finish your workout in the morning, you can fast until noon without losing muscle tone.

The last mistake people often make is to avoid prolonged fasting.

The deeper the fast, the greater the benefit. If you are practicing intermittent fasting for the first time, don't follow it for a long time; however, there are upsides to prolonged fasting. Here are what they are:

- Reduced weight: the body burns stored fat (more of it if you don't eat for up to 20 hours) and automatically reduces your calorie intake. You will not be able to overeat during the time window you set (and you will be more flexible in choosing what you eat).
- Improve insulin sensitivity: insulin sensitivity regulates blood sugar levels, and fasting makes your body more efficient.
- Autophagy: The body initiates cellular repair and recycles old, damaged proteins through a process called autophagy. This usually happens with longer fasts.
- Focus mode: your brain protects neurons, so you feel hyper-focused and stress-resistant.
- Reduction of inflammation: many studies have been conducted in recent years linking fasting to the reduction of inflammation.

# Tips for Intermittent Fasting

To help you along this path and to get the most out of your fasting periods without you having to suffer particularly, I have collected what I believe to be the most important tips for those who decide to start this practice. These things I am about to tell you have in fact had a very positive effect on me, which is why I decided to share them with you.

Definitely the first thing I would tell you if you are approaching fasting for the first time is to fast from evening to morning.

By starting a post-dinner fast, you can spend most of the fast in the evening and after-dinner hours and can then want to fall asleep early. This is advantageous for 2 main reasons:

- By spending much of the time sleeping you will accuse the fasting hours less;
- You can't be hungry while you sleep.

Other advice is to eat foods that satiate you a lot, which is precisely why I have given you a proper eating plan, and you can read some ketogenic recipes that you can prepare quickly and that will help you maintain satiety.

Eating hearty foods with each serving will help you increase the time you feel full after eating, which means you will spend less time feeling hungry.

Good and hearty foods include:

- Potatoes in moderate quantities

- Greek zero-fat yogurt
- Eggs
- Bananas
- Oatmeal
- Soups

Being busy is the perfect way to get rid of constant thoughts of food. Think about how many times boredom has led to one of the following scenarios?

Work proceeds slowly, and you go to the cupboard to get snacks, or in the kitchen you open the refrigerator and eat just to pass the time, or just to take a break from work.

You watch Netflix at home and without thinking about it, almost automatically, you grab snacks, or cookies and various treats to munch on.

If you want to stick to your calorie reduction goal, instead find fun activities or immerse yourself in the work to be done, not only will time pass much faster, but you will also become much more productive.

You should try to manage hunger rather than prevent it during fasting.

I mean, it's okay to feel hungry during fasting, but the goal is to figure out how to overcome that feeling rather than thinking it doesn't exist.

One of the best ways to do this during fasting is to reduce appetite with zero-calorie drinks.

Fasting is not an excuse to eat whatever you want. If you want to lose weight, you still need to create and maintain a calorie deficit. This means that it is important to break the fast with normal amounts of food and especially that it is not junk food.

The last piece of advice I want to give you but which has actually turned out to be very important for me is to plan ahead. Planning ahead and being organized makes intermittent fasting and dieting in general much easier. This is because instead of making a series of small decisions every day, you can just get on with what you need to do.

For example, most people will need to figure out what to eat, when to eat it, when to shop, when to cook, whether it fits their goals, etc.

By doing this work in advance and making decisions in advance, you will simplify the process and reduce the number of decisions you have to make. This increases the chances that you will do what you need to *do, rather than* what *you want to do.*

In the context of a diet, this can mean:

- Start and end fasting at the same time each day
- Eat the same (or similar) healthy foods every day every day.
- Make a shopping list and buy only what you wrote down
- Set aside time each Sunday to prepare meals for the week

Like any time you start something new, fasting takes some getting used to. This means that you are likely to be hungry during the morning for the first few weeks.

At the same time, it is also normal to slip from time to time and stop fasting a little earlier or start a little later. You don't have to grieve over that, it's normal initially, and it's not that bad since you're certainly not used to eating that way.

Don't berate yourself for not being 100% accurate, for the first few weeks allow yourself a margin for error, you are not perfect and this dietary regimen may initially seem very hard.

In these first few weeks you will be able to figure out for sure which type of intermittent fasting is right for you, whether it is preferable for you to choose a softer, 16/8 or 5/2 version or a more drastic one such as the warrior diet or even the OMAD diet, although I have already informed you of my personal experience and preferences in this regard.

# Ketogenic Diet and Intermittent Fasting, can they be combined?

What is the link between the Ketogenic Diet and Intermittent Fasting?

A superficial examination will reveal no similarities between the ketogenic diet and intermittent fasting, but in fact there are many similarities between the two.

Both methods for weight loss greatly change the classic diet; the keto diet affects your filling, involves increasing fat intake while reducing protein and carbohydrate intake, and intermittent fasting changes mealtimes; each day will be divided into fractions of time for eating and fasting.

The common feature of both is weight loss due to the state of ketosis, when the body receives no carbohydrates and is forced to draw energy from stored fats.

There are only two ways to enter the state of ketosis: fasting and the ketogenic diet.

In theory, a combination of these two techniques will help you lose weight faster, but what happens in practice?

With intermittent fasting, the blood sugar level is lowered, this allows your body to intensify the process of ketosis, the body will consequently burn more fat.

But to get real results, you have to practice intermittent fasting for a certain period of time.

Maintaining a ketogenic diet is not easy, and adding fasting will make it even more difficult.

It is important to note that only healthy people can practice the keto diet and intermittent fasting together or separately.

In cases of epilepsy, diabetes mellitus and other metabolic disorders, both methods will be strictly contraindicated for medical reasons. If 16:8 intermittent fasting is used, meals as you know by now will be eaten for eight hours each day, for example, from 10:00 am to 6:00 pm.

With a combination of intermittent fasting and keto, food intake during these eight hours should correspond to generally accepted nutritional ratios in the ketogenic diet: 60-75% of calories should come from fat, 15-30% from protein, and no more than 5-10% from carbohydrates.

In addition, a prerequisite is the use of healthy foods; the keto diet is often positioned as an opportunity to eat unlimited amounts of cheese and bacon and lose weight, but it is not.

No food can be eaten without restrictions, and bacon is not a very healthy processed meat, rather rather it is low in nutrients.

The ketogenic diet and intermittent fasting are combined techniques that together will accelerate fat burning and allow you to follow a dietary regimen that is sustainable over time.

Similarly, each of the methods is difficult to implement; not everyone will like keto nutrition, just as not everyone can stand intermittent fasting. To begin with, you should master the principles of nutrition with a keto diet and only after these have become part of your daily routine, strengthen the diet with intermittent fasting, so as to give, as already explained a boost i.e., a boost to slimming, and achieve a strengthening of the result in terms of weight loss.

# Recipes for the ketogenic diet to go with intermittent fasting

It is now well known that the ketogenic diet brings many of the same benefits associated with intermittent fasting to our bodies, which is why when they are practiced together most people have found significant benefits, not only concerning weight loss, but also a significant increase in their general state of health. That is why below I will outline some simple recipes for the ketogenic diet, really very easy to make, which will increase your sense of satiety during the hours you are allowed to eat, while at the same time introducing healthy foods.

As for the seasonings to be used I recommend that you always use as a type of salt the HIMALAYA ROSE salt, my recommendation is in fact to buy this type of salt in both the "fine" version of the "coarse" type and substitute it for ordinary table salt.

In fact, Himalayan pink salt is not refined and is never treated with any process where chemicals are used, and it also remains by its nature free of the pollutants that can instead contaminate types of salt that come from seas and oceans.

It also reduces water retention and hypertension because its sodium chloride content is significantly lower than ordinary table salt. So although the cost is a little higher than ordinary salt, it is worth buying.

As for the oil, I recommend that you always use a good evo

oil, that is, extra virgin olive oil, and when I use the abbreviation evo oil it will always be to indicate precisely extra virgin olive oil.

## Quick keto ideas for breakfast

-50 grams of smoked salmon with Philadelphia-type spreadable cheese inside

-1 Greek zero fat yogurt+ whole grain oat muesli+ some strawberries+ chia seeds

-2 omelet eggs with inside made into small pieces two sottilette, or at your choice cook the eggs in a nonstick pan and melt two sottilette on top of the eggs

-A glass of whole milk about 200ml or if you prefer vegetable milk and a small sandwich with bresaola and cream cheese spread

-One whole Greek yogurt + a small sandwich with low-fat ham and a small piece of bread

## Quick lunch ideas:

-Egg salad + arugula + avocado + seeds of

sunflower

-Songino-type salad + 1 chopped avocado + light mozzarella + 5 chopped cherry tomatoes

-1 slice of toasted whole wheat bread + low-fat cheese spread + 2 scrambled eggs and half an avocado

-Arugula salad + boiled shrimp + chopped avocado + sesame

seeds

-1 mozzarella cheese with fresh spinach salad and with chopped ripe cherry tomatoes and sunflower seeds

-Salad with salad of your choice + half a chopped green apple +one stick of celery slices+ white grapes and chopped walnuts

-Steamed or grilled cod with grilled or pan-fried zucchini + half an apple

-Grilled or steamed octopus accompanied by grilled or nonstick eggplant + half a pear

## Quick snack ideas:

-A handful of walnuts or almonds or dried fruits

-1 Greek zero fat yogurt + 1 tablespoon almond or walnut granola or dried fruit or alternatively add 2 tablespoons pomegranate kernels

-2 cubes about 30 g parmesan or grana padano cheese

-1 low-fat zero-fat yogurt + fresh blueberries or chopped strawberries

-1 hard-boiled egg

- 1 celery rib with 30 g cream cheese spread

## Quick dinner ideas:

-A slice of grilled tuna or salmon accompanied by steamed vegetables

-Grilled chicken breast accompanied by green salad + half apple or half pear

-Grilled turkey breast accompanied by grilled radicchio

-2 fish skewers accompanied by mixed salad

-2 chicken skewers accompanied by a plate of boiled asparagus dressed with evo oil and lemon

# Quick and easy recipes for the Ketogenic diet:

## Keto zucchini ham and cheese lasagna

Ingredients:

- 2 large zucchini
- 4 thinly sliced light or thinly sliced cheese 60 g
- 100 g of lean cooked ham
- 100 g light béchamel sauce (you can also use the ready-made one)
- 40 g grated grana padano or reggiano cheese
- 6 tablespoons of tomato sauce
- salt and pepper to taste
- 1 teaspoon of evo oil
- a few leaves of fresh or dried basil

Preparation:

Wash and dry the zucchini and then cut them into very thin slices in the horizontal direction of the zucchini, you can help yourself with a peeler or use a knife that cuts well, arrange them on a plate adding salt and pepper and then cook them in a nonstick pan for a few minutes on each side.

Now arrange the zucchini softened by cooking in a small baking dish previously covered with baking paper, on top of the zucchini then add a few spoonfuls of light béchamel sauce spreading it so as to cover the zucchini, put now on top a layer of slices of cooked ham and then the sliced cheese, with a spoon spread then on top the tomato pulp that you have previously seasoned with a drizzle of oil and salt, and sprinkle it all with grated cheese, garnishing with a few leaves of preferably fresh basil.

If you have leftover ingredients, proceed in the same way by forming another layer.

Bake in a preheated oven at 200 degrees for about 20 minutes, until you see a golden crust forming on the surface.

Once cooked remove from the oven, and serve them still stringy.

# Turkey soup

Ingredients:

- 40 grams of sliced mushrooms
- 500 ml of broth
- 2 nuts of butter
- ½ rib of celery
- 300 g turkey breast
- 50 g curly cabbage
- parsley
- 1 clove of garlic
- ½ white onion
- salt and pepper

Preparation:

Wash and chop the celery, garlic, and onion into *brunoise*, then melt the butter in a large saucepan and let the sauté stew over low heat.

Clean and cut the savoy cabbage then divide the leaves and slice them into strips or squares. Add the savoy cabbage to the sauté and stir, add the mushrooms as well and cook for a few min on a moderate flame with a lid.

Cut the turkey breast into 1 cm cubes then add it to the saucepan, pour in the broth and season with salt and pepper. Let the soup cook about 15-20 min on medium heat and finally add chopped parsley. Let the soup rest 5 min. before serving!

Turkey soup is a very flexible recipe, if you prefer you can add a green leafy vegetable of your choice or use chicken breast.

If you prefer a vegetarian soup, simply replace the meat with tofu or include another type of vegetable such as leek or kale!

# Shrimp leek hazelnut salad

Ingredients:

- 12 shrimp tails
- 1 leek
- 12 hazelnuts
- dried chili pepper pieces
- 2 tablespoons soybean sprouts
- 10 fresh cherry tomatoes
- fresh thyme
- pink pepper

Preparation:

First blanch the shrimp tails in a pan with extra virgin olive oil and chili pepper for a few moments then season with salt and pepper and set the tails aside in a bowl.

Wash the leek and cut it into half-inch rounds then stew it in the same pan you cooked the shrimp in with 1 tablespoon of evo oil for a few min. until it becomes soft and translucent. Be careful not to burn the leek so stew it over a low flame.

Wash and cut the cherry tomatoes in half and chop the hazelnuts and thyme with a knife then combine all the ingredients in a boule, add the soybean sprouts and season with salt, pepper and chopped fresh thyme.

Let the salad season 10 min. in the refrigerator and serve!

If you want, you can substitute any other fish for shrimp: shrimp, scallops, squid, or cuttlefish!

# Bresaola keto baskets with cream cheese

Ingredients:

- 150 g bresaola
- 100 g cow's ricotta cheese,
- 100 g robiola cheese,
- 1 tablespoon grated Parmesan cheese,
- chopped parsley and basil
- Pitted green olives to taste.
- a few basil leaves,
- salt and pepper

Preparation:

Drain the ricotta so that the watery part is lost, then in a bowl mix the robiola, ricotta and grated grana cheese. Add the salt and pepper. Now add the chopped herbs to the mixture and mix well, then take the bresaola slices and fill each slice with a little of the cheese mousse.

Stick the slice on one side with a toothpick then add the olive and close the basket by sticking the other side of the bresaola slice.

Continue until you run out of ingredients, you can accompany the dish with mixed salad.

# Parmesan keto pies on tomato sauce

Ingredients for 4 cupcakes:

- 2 eggs
- 100 g grated grana padano or parmesan cheese
- 1 tablespoon of flour about 10 g
- 120 ml of cream
- 50 ml of milk
- salt and pepper to taste
- For the sauce:
- 10 tablespoons of fresh tomato sauce
- 1 level tablespoon of evo oil
- salt and pepper to taste
- half onion
- fresh basil leaves

Preparation:

Put the cream in a nonstick saucepan and dilute it with a tablespoon of water, then add the flour stirring well always in the same direction being careful not to let lumps form, add a pinch of salt and bring to a boil.

Whisk the whole eggs and slowly add the Parmesan cheese, then add the cream previously brought to a boil, to the egg and cheese mixture.

Then fill disposable aluminum molds previously greased well, preferably with a little butter or olive oil.

Place the 4 aluminum ramekins in a baking dish previously filled 2/3 full with 'water and bake in a bain-marie oven at 180 degrees for about 25 minutes.

For the sauce lightly wilt the onion in a small nonstick pan with oil and a trickle of water, add the tomato sauce salt and pepper if you like and basil and cook for 10 minutes, diluting with water.

When cooked, arrange a few spoonfuls of sauce on the plates underneath and then invert the cupcakes, being careful not to break them when removing them from the molds, serve them piping hot garnishing with a few leaves of fresh basil to taste.

# Spinach keto pies with parmesan cream

Ingredients for 4 cupcakes:

- 300 g spinach
- 2 whole eggs
- nutmeg
- 50 g grated cheese or grana padano or parmesan cheese
- 10 g pine nuts
- 1 tablespoon of milk, including vegetable milk
- 1 tablespoon of evo oil
- salt and pepper to taste

For the cream:

- 50 g grated cheese or grana padano or parmesan cheese
- 130 ml of semi-skimmed milk or vegetable if you prefer
- 15 g of 00 flour
- 10 g butter

Preparation:

Boil the spinach until fully cooked, drain it in a colander with the help of a spoon so that all the cooking water is completely removed and let it cool. Once cooled put them in a bowl and add the eggs, nutmeg the Parmesan cheese and pine nuts and mix everything well, diluting with a little milk and helping yourself if you prefer with a food processor.

Coat 4 disposable aluminum molds well with oil and pour the mixture inside, bake in a bain-marie by placing the molds in a pan filled 2/3 full of water at 180 degrees for about 25 minutes.

For the parmesan cream:

Heat the milk on the stove without letting it boil, separately heat the butter by adding the flour without forming lumps, and then gradually add the hot milk so that everything is well mixed.

Cook the mixture created over medium-low heat until it begins to thicken, at which point gradually add the grated cheese and continue stirring, creating a smooth cream.

When cooked, arrange the cream in the center of the plate and place the spinach flan on top, cover the flans by pouring the remaining cream over them, and serve piping hot.

# Pumpkin keto flans with goat cheese cream

Ingredients for 4 cupcakes:

- 400 g of pumpkin pulp
- 2 whole eggs
- nutmeg
- 50 g grated grana padano or parmesan cheese
- 10 g pine nuts
- 2 tablespoons of milk, including vegetable milk
- ½ onion
- 1 tablespoon of evo oil
- salt and pepper to taste
- For the cream:
- 200 g of goat cheese
- 100 ml of fresh liquid light cream
- salt and pepper to taste

Preparation:

in a saucepan, melt the butter with the sliced onion and the pumpkin flesh, previously cleaned of seeds and diced, adding a ladleful of hot water, cooking until the pumpkin flakes off, becoming soft but remaining rather dry and not watery; it will take about 20 to 25 minutes to cook completely.

Transfer the puree to a bowl and once cooled add the eggs, nutmeg the Parmesan cheese the pine nuts salt and pepper and mix everything well, diluting with a little milk to blend and help yourself if you prefer with a food processor.

Coat 4 disposable aluminum molds well with oil, pour the mixture inside, bake in a bain-marie by placing the molds in a pan filled 2/3 full of water at 180 degrees for about 35 minutes.

For the goat cheese cream:

in a bowl pour the goat cheese and cream cheese and salt and pepper, whisk with a hand or electric whisk to create a creamy mixture so that everything is well blended.

When the pumpkin flans are cooked, arrange the cream in the center of the dish and place the flan on top, being careful to remove it from the ramekin without breaking it, then cover it by pouring over the remaining cream, and serve piping hot.

# Keto chicken chunks with feta and zucchini

Ingredients:

- 150 gr chicken
- 60 gr diced feta cheese
- 1 zucchini
- 4 basil leaves
- oil, salt and pepper

Preparation:

Cut the chicken into cubes about 1/2 inch thick and place in a bowl to marinate with a drizzle of oil, a pinch of salt pepper and chopped basil leaves. Let stand for about 10 minutes or so.

Cut the zucchini into rounds that are not too thin and brown it in a pan for 6 to 8 minutes with a drizzle of oil and a pinch of salt.

Cook the chicken by sautéing it in a nonstick skillet until it is lightly browned.

Arrange in a cube dish creating a bed of zucchini then joining the chicken cubes and feta, add a drizzle of raw evo oil to taste.

# Keto zucchini stuffed with meat and cheese

Ingredients for 2 persons:

- 4 Round zucchini (or regular zucchini)
- 200 g of lean mince
- 50 gr of grana padano cheese
- 30 gr of Pecorino Romano cheese
- 30 g breadcrumbs
- 1 bunch of fresh basil
- 1 whole egg
- 1 clove of garlic minced if liked
- 1 pinch of salt

Preparation:

Cut off the top cap of the zucchini, empty them of their pulp and set aside.

Blanch the zucchini in salted boiling water for a few minutes, they should be soft but not flaky, then drain and lay them on top of a clean tea towel and let cool. In a bowl combine the whole egg previously beaten with a fork, add salt a drizzle of oil, parmesan and pecorino cheese, breadcrumbs and garlic if you like, also add the shredded zucchini flesh, and chopped basil, with your hands or with a mixer create a thick mixture with which to stuff the zucchini.

Stuff the zucchini and bake at 200 degrees for about 30 minutes. Remove from the oven and let cool a few minutes before serving.

# Omelet with mushrooms squash blossoms and asparagus

Ingredients:

- 4 eggs
- 5 squash blossoms
- 2 asparagus
- 4 champignon mushrooms
- ½ onion
- 1 tablespoon parmesan cheese
- 1 tablespoon grated parmesan cheese
- fresh basil
- 3 nuts of ghee butter
- salt and pepper

Preparation:

Clean the mushrooms by stripping them of the dirty part of the stem and slice them into half-inch slices, cut the onion into julienne and brown it in a pan over moderate heat, add the mushrooms and cook them for a few minutes with a lid on.

Peel the asparagus stalks and then cut them into pieces as you prefer, 2-3 cm rounds or sticks. Steam the asparagus for about 7 min.

Clean the squash blossoms by removing the inner pistil and cut them in half lengthwise.

Whisk eggs in a bowl along with salt, pepper, Parmesan cheese and basil leaves. Add the asparagus to the mushrooms in the pan and then pour in the beaten eggs. On top of the eggs, lay the squash blossoms evenly then reduce the heat to low and cover.

Cook until the egg has set then turn the omelet over with the help of a plate and serve hot with a sprinkling of grated Parmesan cheese!

The omelet is also great with artichoke hearts instead of asparagus or by substituting champignons for porcini mushrooms, try it!

# Baked salmon with boiled asparagus

Ingredients for 2 persons:

- 2 salmon fillets
- 400 g fresh asparagus
- 2 cloves of garlic, minced (if liked)
- 4 tablespoons of evo oil
- black pepper and salt
- lemon juice
- a tuft of chopped parsley
- a few leaves of chopped basil

Preparation:

First prepare the marinade by mixing the minced garlic cloves with the tablespoons of oil, basil black pepper and salt, lemon juice and chopped parsley. Cover the salmon fillets with the marinade and let them rest in the refrigerator for at least an hour, turning them occasionally.

Arrange the fillets on a sheet of baking paper, cover them with the marinade, and bake for about 40 minutes in a preheated oven at 180 degrees.In the meantime that the salmon is baking in the oven, boil the asparagus for about 5 minutes until softened, and season with oil and lemon.Once golden brown in the oven, serve the salmon accompanied by the asparagus.

# Crispy keto cutlet

Ingredients:

- 1 slice of veal 150 g approx.
- 40 g grated parmesan or grana cheese
- 40 g hazelnuts
- 1 whole egg
- evo oil, salt and pepper

Preparation:

Coarsely chop the hazelnuts and combine them with the grated parmesan or grana cheese.

Put the whole egg in a bowl and beat it with a fork and then dip the meat into it on both sides and then later mash it over the parmesan and hazelnut batter.

Heat a nonstick skillet with plenty of evo oil and cook the meat, turning several times, for about 10 minutes. Dry the cutlet from excess oil with kitchen paper.

Serve hot after salting and accompany with grilled zucchini or eggplant.

# Baked stringy keto broccoli

Ingredients:

- 2 Broccoli
- 30 g of slivered almonds
- 3 tablespoons Olive oil
- Salt and pepper to taste
- 2 pieces of chopped thinner
- 30 g grated parmesan or grana cheese
- one clove of garlic, minced if liked

Preparation:

Cut the broccoli into florets, then wash them under running water and blanch them for 5 minutes in boiling salted water. Drain and let cool, then grease an ovenproof dish with oil and lay the broccoli seasoned with salt, pepper and a drizzle of olive oil and garlic if you like.

Then sprinkle the surface with grated parmesan or grana cheese and chopped sottilette add almond slivers and bake in a 200°C oven for 20 minutes.

# Baked keto crushes

Ingredients for 6 pieces:

- 220 g mozzarella for pizza
- 60 g Philadelphia
- 40 g sliced green or black olives
- 1 teaspoon baking powder for savory
- 2 whole eggs
- 50 g of slivered almonds

Preparation:

Beat the whole eggs with a fork and add the slivered almonds the olives and the baking powder and mix everything together.

Melt the mozzarella and Philadelphia cheese in the microwave for 2 minutes and add them to the eggs with the olives and almonds and add the baking powder and mix well.

Create 6 crushes with the dough and place them spaced apart on a baking sheet and bake at 200 degrees for about 20 minutes.

# Ham nests with spinach and eggs

Ingredients:

- 4 slices of cured ham
- 2 large eggs
- 70 g spinach
- 2 tablespoons of cottage cheese
- fresh chives
- 1 tablespoon grated parmesan cheese
- pine nuts

Preparation:

Clean the spinach and boil it 2 min in salted water then drain, squeeze out excess water and chop it with a knife. Transfer the spinach to a bowl and add the ricotta, eggs, chopped chives and pine nuts.

Mix to make a homogeneous filling then take molds and line them with slices of ham (I recommend dividing each slice in half so that the hollow is lined with the two parts overlapping) in the center add the mixture with a spoon, top with Parmesan cheese and bake at 180° for about 13 min. or until you see the egg has set. Serve the nests either hot or cold!

If you don't like cottage cheese you can also use mascarpone cheese, and if you don't like spinach try replacing it with broccoli or turnip greens!

# Yogurt and blueberry keto mousse

Ingredients:

- 200 ml whipping cream
- 170 g white Greek or berry yogurt
- 100 g of blueberries
- sweetener to taste stevia or erythrole

Preparation:

Heat blueberries for a couple of minutes with a couple of tablespoons of water and add sweetener to your taste. Remove from heat and blend with a minipimer type immersion blender and let cool.

In the meantime, whip the cream with electric whips and add the Greek yogurt; once it has reached a consistent, creamy density, also add the blueberry mixture gently, stirring lightly until a mousse is created.

Pour into 4 cups and let cool in the refrigerator before serving.

# Cocoa and almond mascarpone cream

Ingredients:

- 3 egg yolks
- 2 egg whites
- 250 g mascarpone
- 5 drops of sweetener (tic or other type)
- bitter cocoa powder
- slivered almonds

Preparation:

Whip the egg yolks with the mascarpone and sweetener, then separately whip the egg whites to stiff peaks and add them, stirring gently into the previous mixture.

Arrange the cream in 4 small cups and sprinkle with bitter cocoa and sprinkle a few slivers of peeled almonds on top. Chill the cups in the refrigerator and serve cold.

# Porridge with cinnamon and dried fruit

Ingredients:

- 300 ml almond milk
- 3 tablespoons chia seeds
- 2 tablespoons unsweetened coconut flakes
- 1 tablespoon of almond flour
- 5 walnuts
- 5 almonds
- 5 hazelnuts
- 1 tablespoon coconut flour
- 1 teaspoon cinnamon powder

Preparation:

Pour the milk into a saucepan and add the flours by sifting them, heat the milk for about 4-5 min. and stir to avoid creating lumps, then turn off.

Chop all the dried fruit and combine it with the milk with the chia seeds and coconut flakes, then transfer the mixture to two small bowls. Serve the porridge hot sprinkled with cinnamon powder!

If you want you can prepare the oatmeal a day ahead and let it rest overnight in the refrigerator, this way you will get a delicious overnight oat to enjoy for breakfast!

# Exercises to keep fit

Below I propose some simple exercises that you can do at home to keep your body moving and healthy, resulting in the awakening of your metabolism, in fact, doing physical activity increases energy expenditure, all of which will then go together with the beneficial effects of your new eating plan, resulting in an even greater improvement in lean mass at the expense of fat mass, to achieve even more easily the goal you have set for yourself, to get back in shape while remaining healthy at the same time. I must tell you, however, that when training and practicing intermittent fasting, it is good to keep in mind that, as I have already anticipated in previous chapters, it would be best to plan your workouts before the largest meal of the day, preferably in the morning if your schedule allows, starting gradually to give your body time to get used to it.

I offer below simple exercises that you can do in sequence or separately to strengthen and tone all the muscles in your body.

You can repeat the sequences one or more times depending on your endurance or going then to increase them over time to intensify the workout.

# Firming buttocks

I believe that having a high and firm butt is everyone's dream, and having a toned one is not impossible, in fact, you just need to do the right exercises to firm the buttocks, let's find out some of them together.

## Rear gluteal slumps

You can do this exercise either free-body or you may also choose to do it with weighted ankle straps or elastic bands, clearly increasing the effort and energy expenditure. Get on all fours and sprawl one bent leg backward with your hammer foot while maintaining a straight line with your back: then raise your leg over the line of your back and bring it back to the starting position. Repeat the exercise in sets of 15 2 times per leg.

## Lateral gluteal slumps

Lie on your side and rest your head on the arm that is on the ground. Bring your other arm to your side then raise your leg up and lower it without letting it touch the leg that is on the ground. Do 10 sets then switch sides and alternate leg and repeat for 3 sets.

# Gluteal pelvis lift

Stand on the floor with your arms along your body and bend your legs, leaving the soles of your feet in contact with the floor. Then raise your pelvis upward so that your body has a triangular shape and leave your shoulders attached to the floor. Lower your pelvis without letting your butt touch the floor and then raise again. Do repetitions of 15 for 3 times.

# Inner Thigh Exercises

This is a specific workout for the inner thigh, to make it even more effective I use weighted ankle straps, but if you don't have them at home you can easily perform it without them.

The inner thigh is a trouble spot for some of us, but fear not, these are all simple and very functional exercises.

## Exercise from lying down inner thigh

Lie on the floor on a mat and lie on your right side, with your right elbow resting on the floor and your hand supporting your head. Bend your left leg and place your foot and ground behind your right knee.

Lift the outstretched right leg up and down while keeping the toe of the foot at the hammertoe and then alternate the exercise on the other side.

Do the exercise for 15 lunges and repeat 2 times per side.

# Legs up open and close for inner thighs

We continue firming the inner thigh with this other exercise.

Lie on the floor with your arms along your sides and bring your legs together stretched upward. Open and close your legs while keeping them extended. If you can, stand near a wall and move a few inches away from the wall with your pelvis and legs. Repeat 10 times the lunges for 2 sets.

# Arm workout

Here are some exercises for the arms, which are in fact like the abs and buttocks a part of the body that we all dream of having toned, in fact unfortunately it is often the first to suffer the consequences of weight gain or low physical activity, it also suffers a significant loss of tone as we age.

## Arm workout with chair

This dedicated upper body workout makes use of a chair.

In fact, to tone the arms, we do not always need large weights or special equipment; our own body weight is more than enough.

Rest your palms on the edge of the chair and put your legs in front of you with your feet resting well on the floor.

Bend your arms and go with your pelvis toward the ground as far as you can while being careful not to arch your back, which should remain as straight as possible. Repeat the exercise for 10 squats for 2 sets.

## Arm workout with small weights

Here is another very simple arm-firming exercise that can be performed with small weights that you can find at Decathlon or many other sports stores, or even simple full water bottles are fine.

Start by standing with legs spread at pelvic height and knees slightly flexed.

Grasp the weights or water bottles with a firm grip and keep your arms extended. From this position, bend them toward your chest while keeping your elbows steady and then stretch them downward again.

As you perform the entire exercise strive to keep your back straight and your abs contracted to protect your lower back. Breathe in and out regularly and do not hold your breath, and perform the movements slowly. Do 3 sets of 10 repetitions.

# Abs workout

The abdominals are a weak point for almost all of us as we often end up with an unsightly tummy, solving this problem may seem difficult but it is not impossible, so I propose abdominal exercises aimed at obtaining a flatter and toned abdomen that will improve even more by following the food plan recommended here, so much so that it will become a real healthier and more effective lifestyle to achieve the desired results.

## Lateral abs

Lie on your side with legs outstretched. Place your elbow on the floor and your open hand on the floor. Lift yourself up by levering your side abdominal muscles and bringing your body up all at once. Now stay in this position keeping the muscles contracted for one minute and then come back down. Repeat remaining in the contracted position 3 times.

## Bicycle floor workout

Lie down with your back on the ground and lift your legs up to simulate when you are pedaling a bicycle. Keep your arms along your sides and try never to touch the ground with your heels. This will contract your abdominal muscles, which will begin to work. Do the exercise for a few minutes.

# Pillow abdominal workout

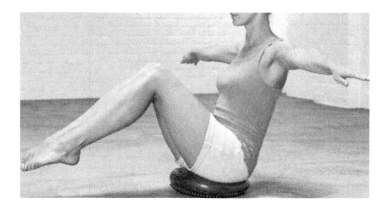

To develop balance and endurance, yielding tools are useful, even a simple pillow we have at home can be fine, alternatively you can buy soft rubber unstable bases like the one you see in the photo, which help us counteract body imbalance and maintain correct posture.

The work is on balance, so the abs are strengthened, but this exercise also comprehensively involves the entire body musculature.

Sit on the pillow and take your legs and feet off the floor and balance, stand still with your arms outstretched by pulling your abdominal muscles and holding the position as long as you can.

There are many ways to activate your metabolism, a very good way is to do it by keeping yourself moving with the right exercises like the ones I have given you some examples of above, you can then over time increase the number of sets to make your metabolism burn more and more.

You can also vary the type of workout you do, such as going for a run sometimes or using the exercise bike or treadmill or going for a brisk walk outdoors, so that your metabolism is forced to adapt to different physical training situations.

You can still change the times you work out to keep your body from getting used to the same rhythms all the time.

All this is to create a strong synergy between the new eating plan you will adopt by following the ketogenic diet and intermittent fasting, and physical movement, which will make achieving your goal of getting back in shape fast, soon a quick reality.

# Conclusions

Intermittent fasting along with exercise, allowed me to get back into shape particularly during the lock down period when forced closures, smart working, and constant access to the kitchen and refrigerator had made me noticeably heavier and lose the fitness I had gained in the past by practicing alternating periods of rest with my favorite diets, which are the ketogenic diet, the sirt diet, and the low carb diet.

In a short time I was able to achieve results that only until recently I thought were unattainable. This diet stimulated me immediately, because it presented itself profoundly different from any other. The results, however, from the very first moment I can say with certainty that they were truly incredible.

One thing I think is crucial, however, before starting intermittent fasting is to focus on your mindset, i.e., your state of mind: if in fact you are afraid that you will not last a day without eating sweets or junk food and this prevents you from starting a diet, try not to eat this food, to completely erase it from your days and face your fear, take it head on. If you are afraid to join a gym because you fear being judged, do it, join, don't waste any more time. In fact, your fears every time they are confronted, they shrink.

Also know that in order to stay clear-headed and in control of your actions, it becomes essential to sleep regularly. You should sleep an average of 7-8 hours a day. Sleeping even one hour less each day, leads you in the long run to be much more stressed and therefore less clear-headed to better handle difficulties, that's why among the forms of intermittent fasting I told you about my favorite is the 16/8 form of fasting, because you can devote in a healthy way hours to our rest and at the same time by sleeping we will feel less hunger and lack of food. When you start a new diet you may probably encounter several difficulties, which is precisely why you need to be mentally clear to deal with them as best you can. Try to keep a regular schedule so that your brain can maintain a good circadian rhythm, that is, the rhythm of your 24 hours a day.

If you want to be in control of your life at all times you should reduce both alcohol and as I suggested earlier, also not abuse caffeine. Surely coffee can be useful for you to wake up in the morning and activate your body and sometimes you will need it to buffer your sense of hunger, but taking it in excessive amounts is wrong, and it does not benefit your body at all. Alcohol also allows you to relax however you should eliminate it completely or almost completely from your diet.

When you buy only the foods and beverages that are really useful for your diet, you will find that you will also be able to save a lot of money. When this happens you live your life in a better way, you can in fact treat yourself to something you enjoy, and why not every now and then you might reward yourself by spending the money you save to treat yourself to a nice beauty treatment, such as a nice relaxing massage, a session at the hairdresser, or maybe treat yourself to a nice new dress to wear as soon as you are a little thinner so that it will fit you even better. When you behave this way and spend your money only on the things you actually need, your worries ease, much of the stress goes away altogether. You also begin to prioritize other things, and you are able to find more balance as well, because you don't have to pay attention every time to the single penny you spend more or less while shopping or shopping.

In recent times, people lead a worse lifestyle because they cannot manage their time and so what little time they have they do not want to waste by cooking maybe a good healthy meal. In fact you actually have to know that each person spends from 1 hour up to 3/4 hours every day in using social media, such as Facebook or Instagram, or tik tok or doing reels. These just listed represent the primary way through which people waste their time. In most cases you won't even find interesting topics or notions on social, but there are usually a lot of useless discussions and unhealthy comparisons that only increase nervousness and stress. For these reasons you should minimize your use of them, and spend more time perhaps for a healthy walk in the fresh air or to hear from some of your friends and preferably meet them in person, not just talking to them via whatsapp telegram chat or instagram and facebook.

These socials can yes be considered a useful tool for keeping in touch with people who perhaps at one point in life are far away from you, but you should not use them for other purposes, to waste time, earn that time and employ some of it to cook a tasty dish, or to go grocery shopping and buy healthier, more sought-after products. You can also use the time saved to keep your home and work space neat and organized. Very often without realizing it we live in physical clutter that reflects mental clutter. When you get organized all you do is focus on what you are doing rather than your surroundings. When you act in an organized way, you can notice the first improvements in your lifestyle, you will have more time to focus on the activities that are really important to you, and you will be able to achieve great results in every area of life.

After a short time that you have applied what is said in this book, and also followed the advice that I, who tried it myself before you, felt like giving you, I assure you that you will be able to see the first results on your body. You will have lost some of your fat and, if you also go to the gym or simply perform at home the exercises I have indicated in the appropriate chapter, you will also have gained some muscle. You will look much healthier, and you will benefit not only your physique but also your mind. Achieving the first results through your new eating style will allow you to prove to yourself that you really can achieve any goal. If you have never managed to lose weight before now, doing it once in your life by practicing intermittent fasting will give you greater mastery of your body, greater clarity and will also bring your body a greater sense of well-being, as practicing it also brings, among other benefits, an increase in serotonin, that is, the hormone of happiness.

To change your diet I recommend that you follow the attached eating plan, so do not proceed "by hand" but be aware of what you eat day by day. You have to get organized, so maybe the first period, to proceed better, you will have to write down on a sheet of paper what you are going to eat each day during the hours allotted for meals. This is all very easy to do if you really want to do it. Stop saying you can't do something unless this is physically impossible. Instead of saying you will never do something or that you have other priorities to avoid making an effort, try, really try to change. Change your habit of saying that you "can't" do something. Remove these words from your dictionary, you have to train yourself to think positively and purposefully. You must not immediately think that something you have not done is impossible to do. If you haven't done it and someone has managed to do it, it is probably doable. If you want to keep control of your life, you have to be the one to deal with events and not be overwhelmed by them.

 If you are someone who likes to take on new challenges this is definitely the diet for you. Also don't think that fasting is really impossible for you, initially it will probably seem like an insurmountable feat, or something really very difficult to tackle, I can assure you though that you have all the makings of your best.

After a short time if you follow all the advice and guidance encapsulated in this manual you will realize that following such a dietary regimen is not so hard. In fact, you will probably be able to feel some positive feelings right away. Your body will quickly get used to this diet regimen, because we humans are not made to eat large amounts of food.

If you follow my advice you will no longer be addicted to junk food, or to consuming huge amounts of sweets, you will have a new life in front of you that is certainly much healthier. If you are afraid of this fast, start with the most "acceptable" type, that is, the one in which you are fasting for 16 hours and eat on the other 8. This type does not stray far from a normal diet. For these very reasons, as I have already pointed out to you, you might accept it more easily.

Gradually you will be able to intensify your fasting hours, you will be able to try the various modes and set new goals. You and only you can impose limits on your life, and likewise you are the only person who may be able to break them down.

Sure, sometimes you may feel lonely and lost in your journey, your goals may seem very far away or even unattainable. The reality is that you can achieve any goal if you want to. You can shape your physique any way you like, you can lose weight and reach your goal weight even if you have always thought that this is impossible.

Do not envy other people who enjoy excellent health and are fit but start working on yourself to be like them. Remember that being fit does not only and exclusively mean appearing more pleasing to the eye from the aesthetic side, but above all it means being healthy, avoiding the onset of disease and having a healthier lifestyle.

There are millions of people who have decided to adopt this diet regimen, you could try it too, after all, you have nothing to lose. There is a strong scientific basis behind this diet, and there are plenty of benefits for you. Should you not be happy with it, you can always retrace your steps, however, do not preclude yourself from trying this new diet regimen.

Whenever you feel lonely and misunderstood don't beat yourself up, you have a weapon at your disposal that will accompany you during these weeks, this manual. I have shared with you every bit of my experience so that you can achieve the results you have always dreamed of.

It only remains for me to tell you to 'take action' and not to waste any more time. Don't feel sorry for yourself, it's time to take action, a brighter future in health and fitness awaits you, after all, as the great Jack Canfield said, 'everything you want is on the other side of fear' and so don't delay and act now!

*Best of luck!*

# AUTHOR INFORMATION

Claudia Rodriguez is a professional in the holistic field, specializing in self-help and nutrition, and works as a coach with nutrition counseling and support to help people regain their figure, health, and personal well-being.

Printed in Great Britain
by Amazon

25403118R00106